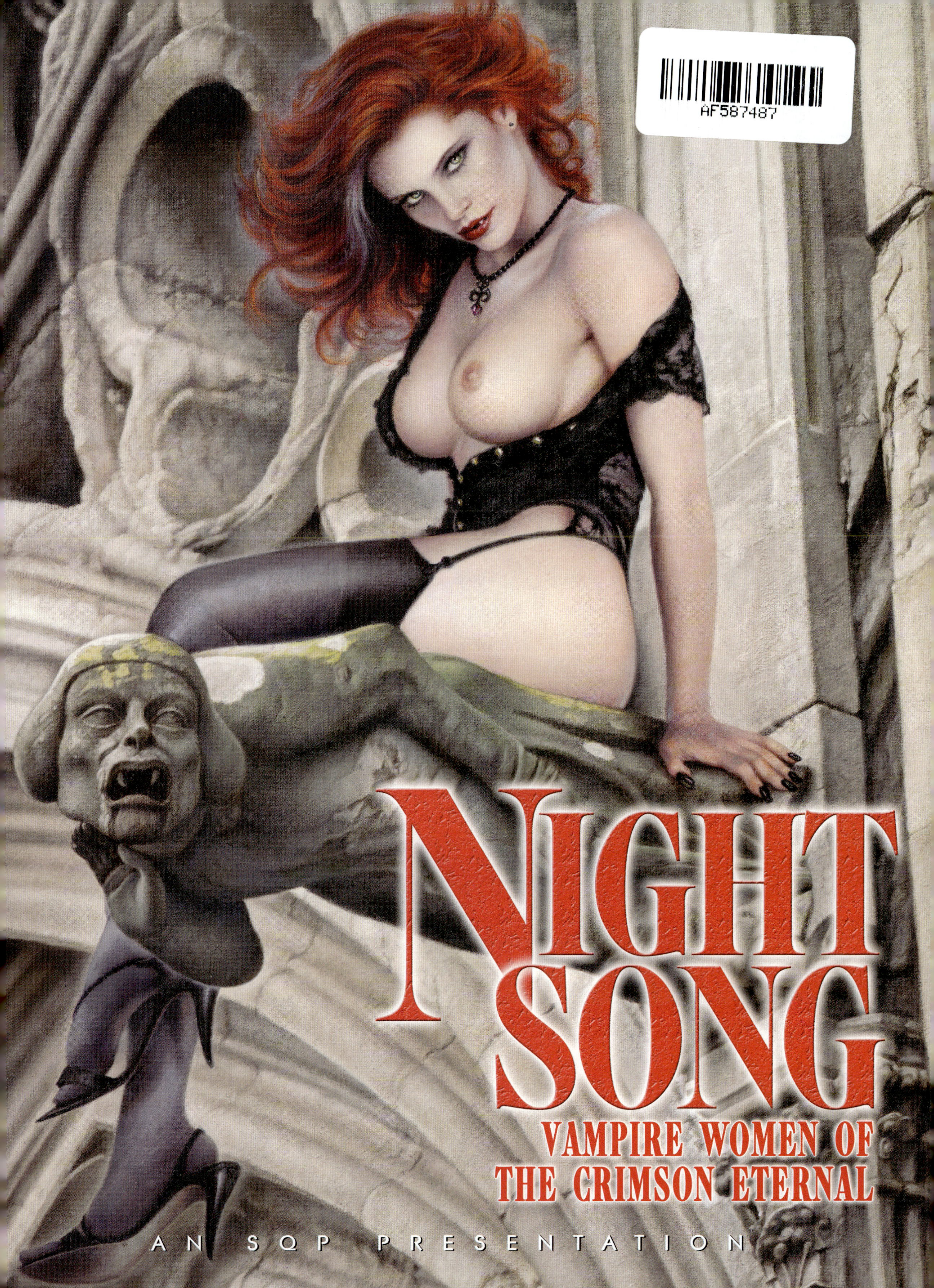

AF587487
NIGHT SONG
VAMPIRE WOMEN OF THE CRIMSON ETERNAL
AN SQP PRESENTATION

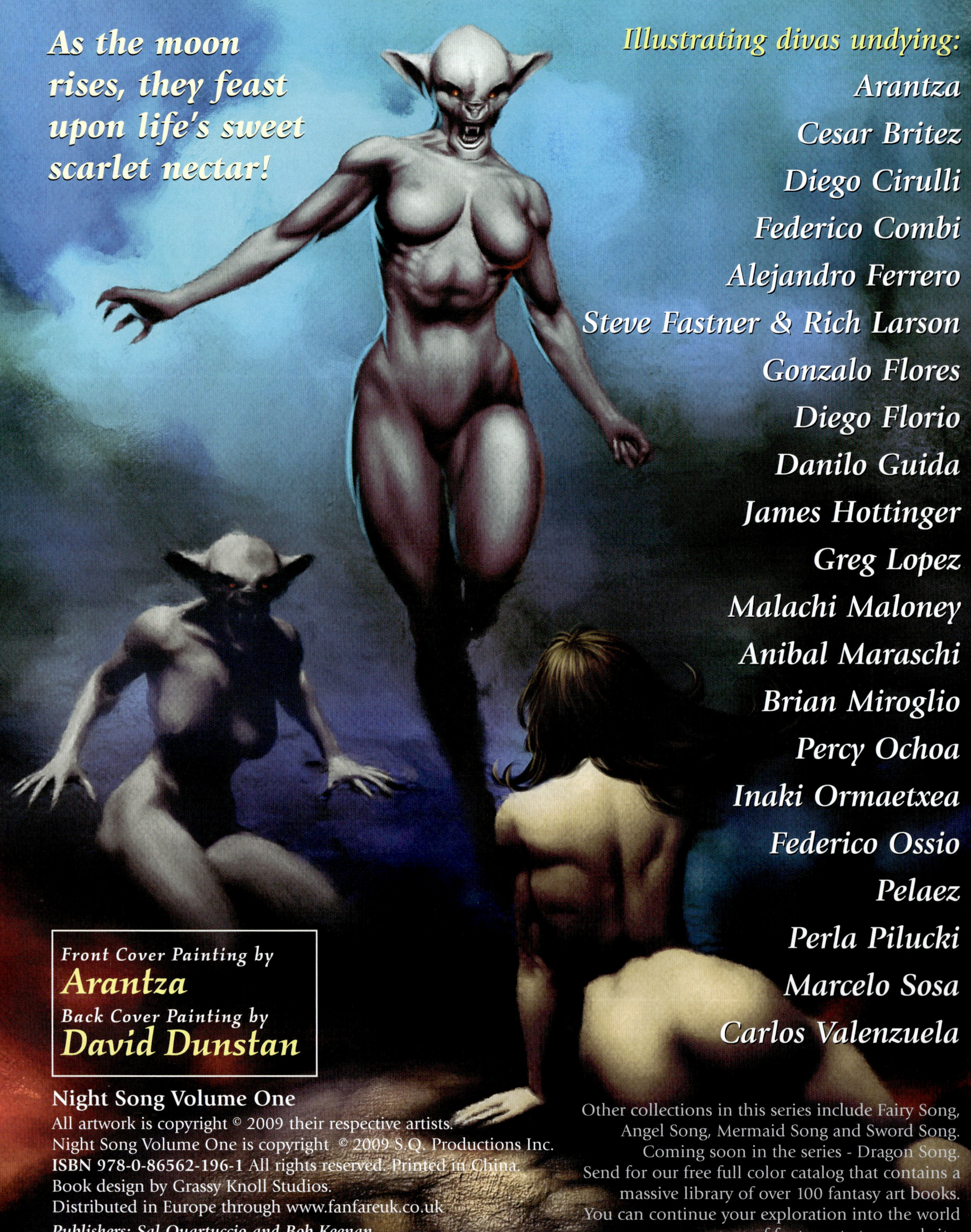

Night Song Volume One

ISBN 978-0-86562-196-1 All rights reserved. Printed in China.
Book design by Grassy Knoll Studios.
Distributed in Europe through www.fanfareuk.co.uk
Publishers: Sal Quartuccio and Bob Keenan
SQP Inc. - PO Box 248 - Columbus, NJ 08022

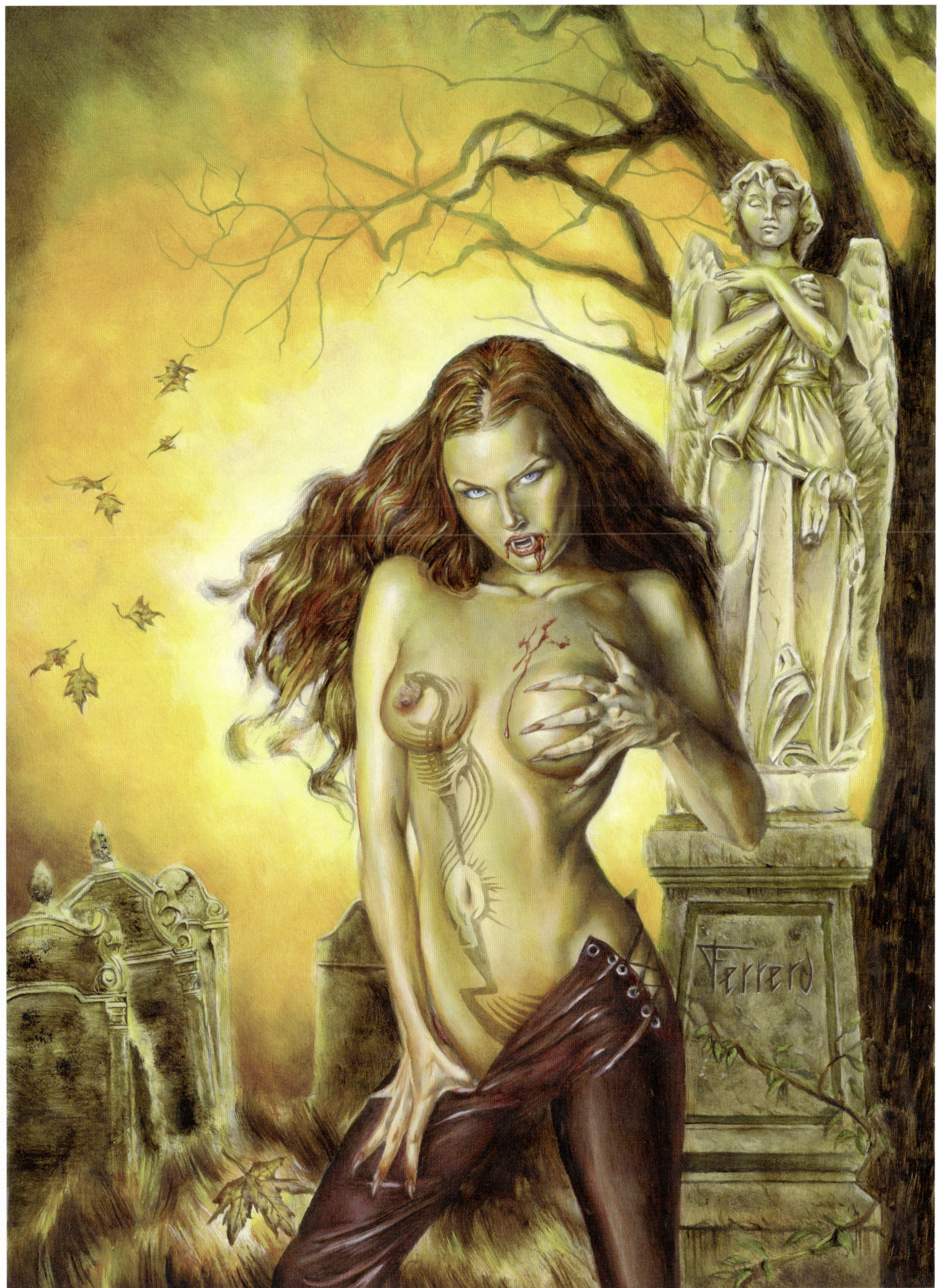

Hunger Eternal

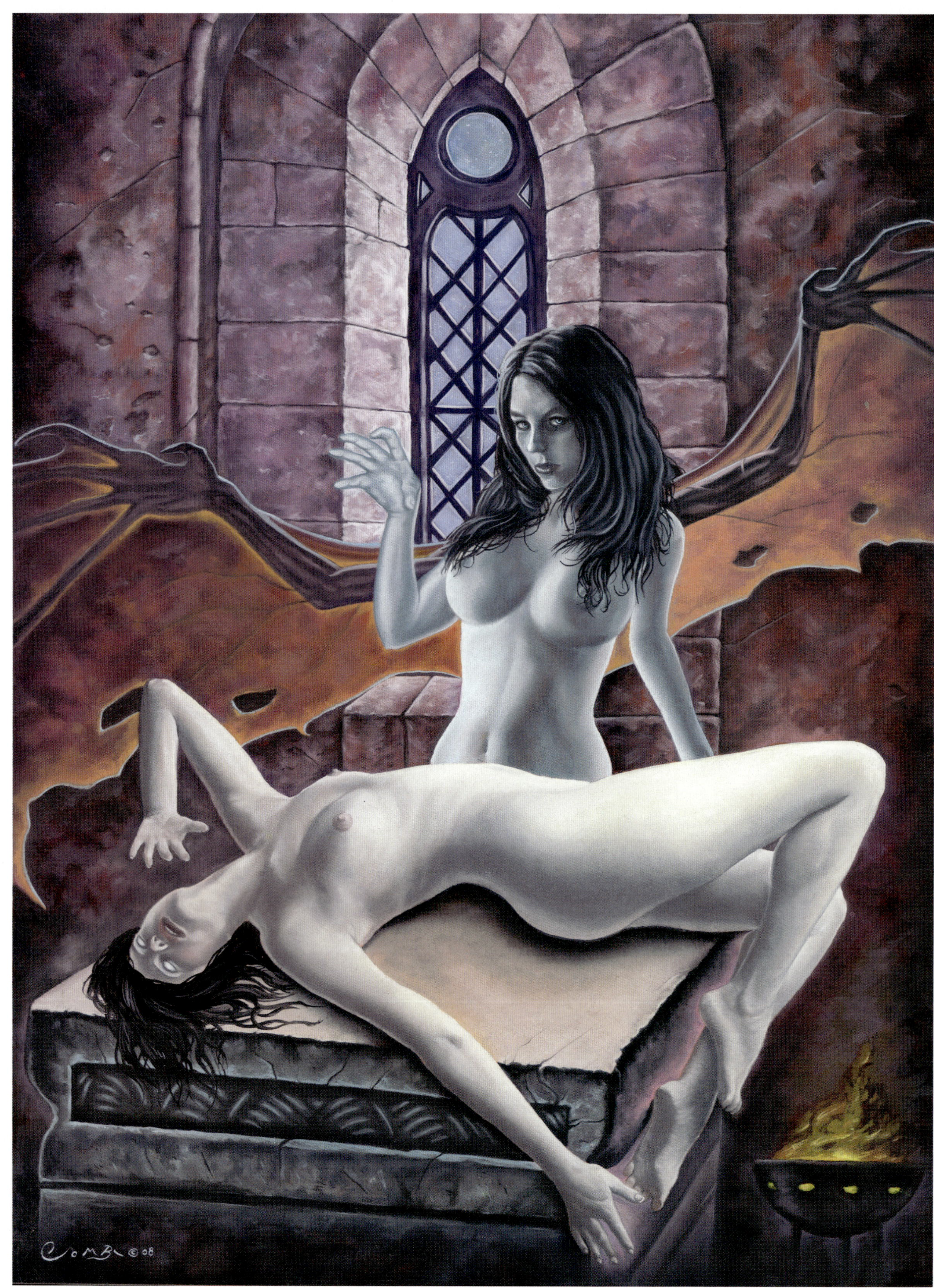

A Love Consumed

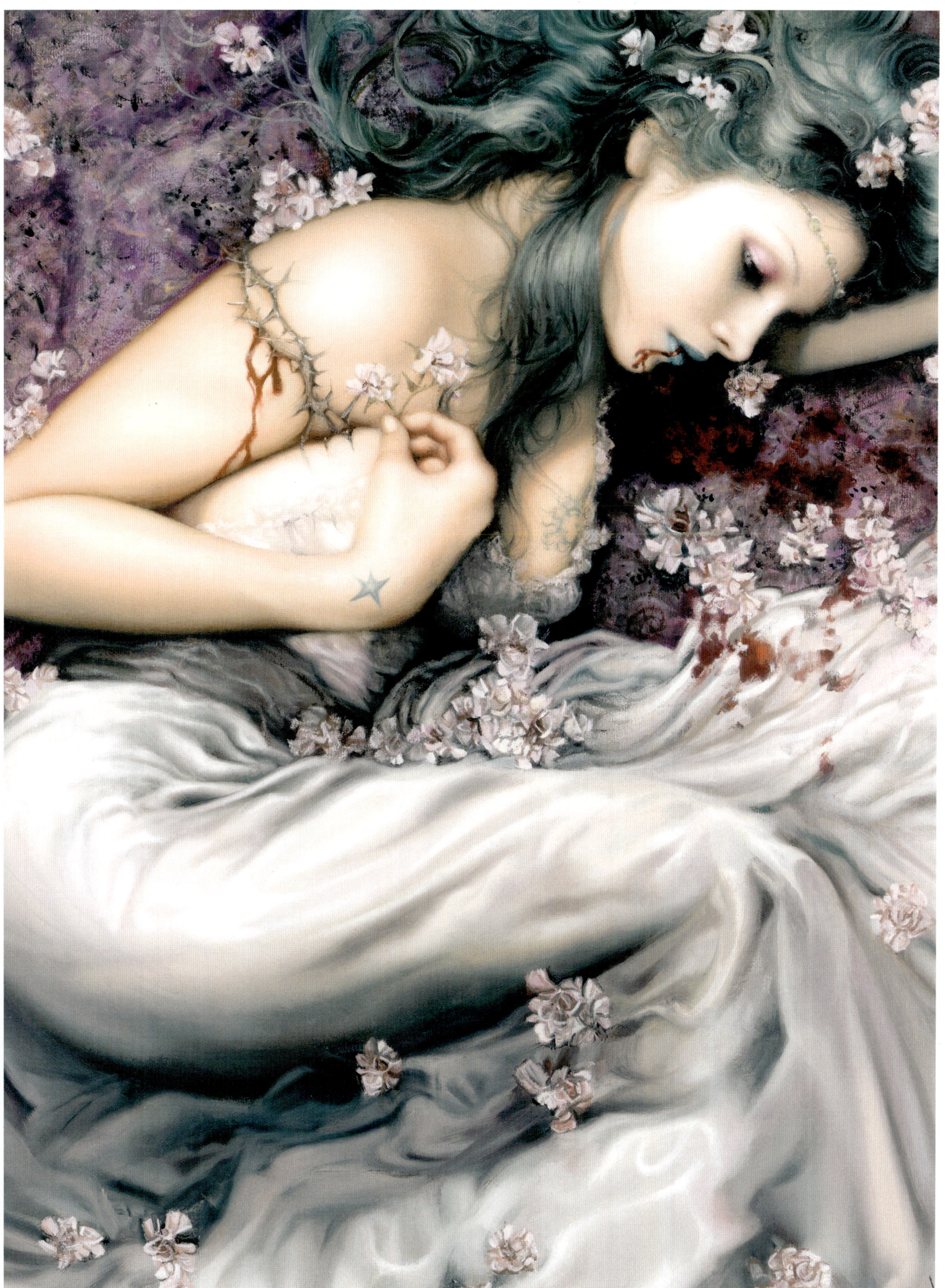

The Comfort of Thorns

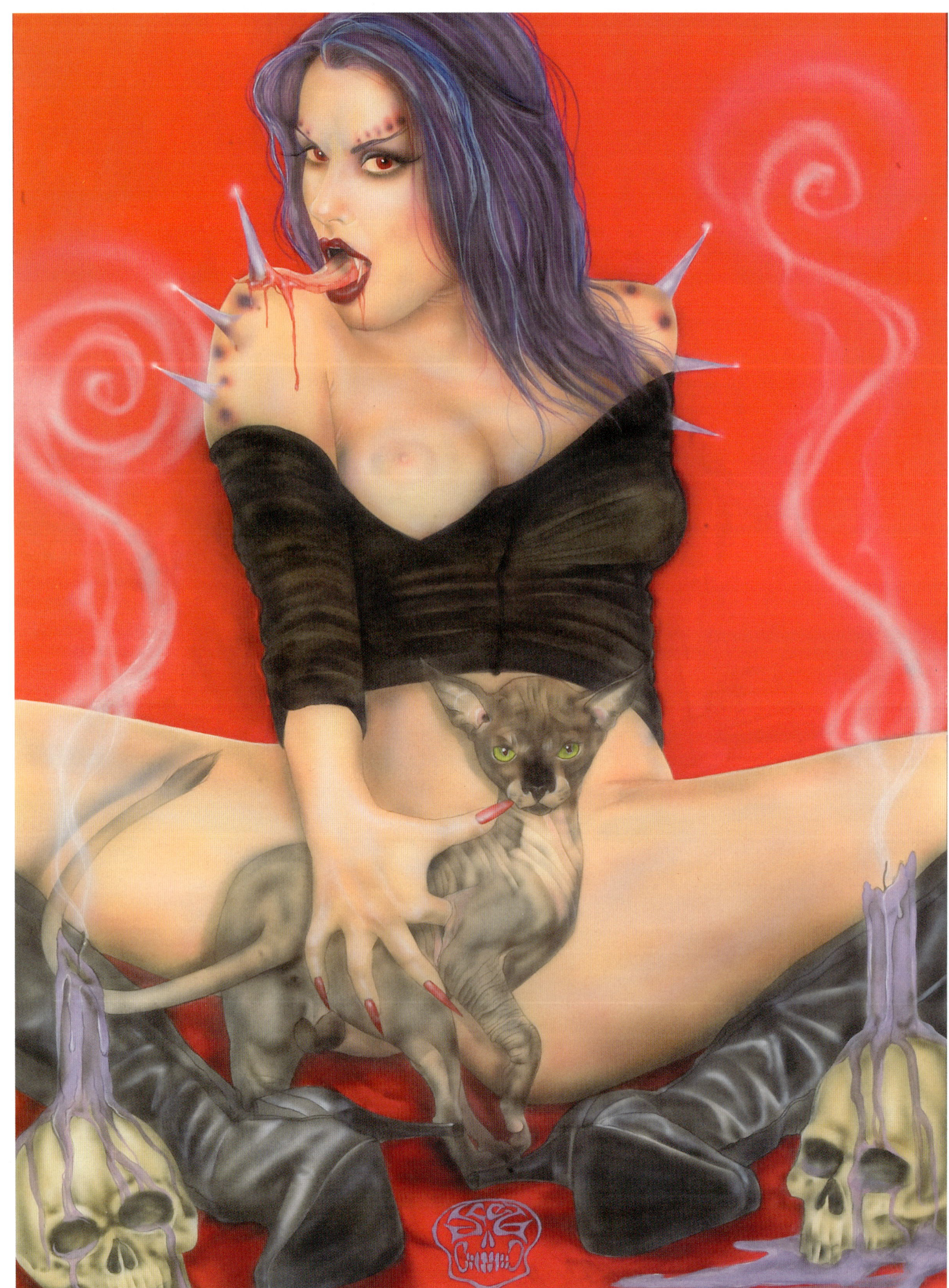

Demon Lust

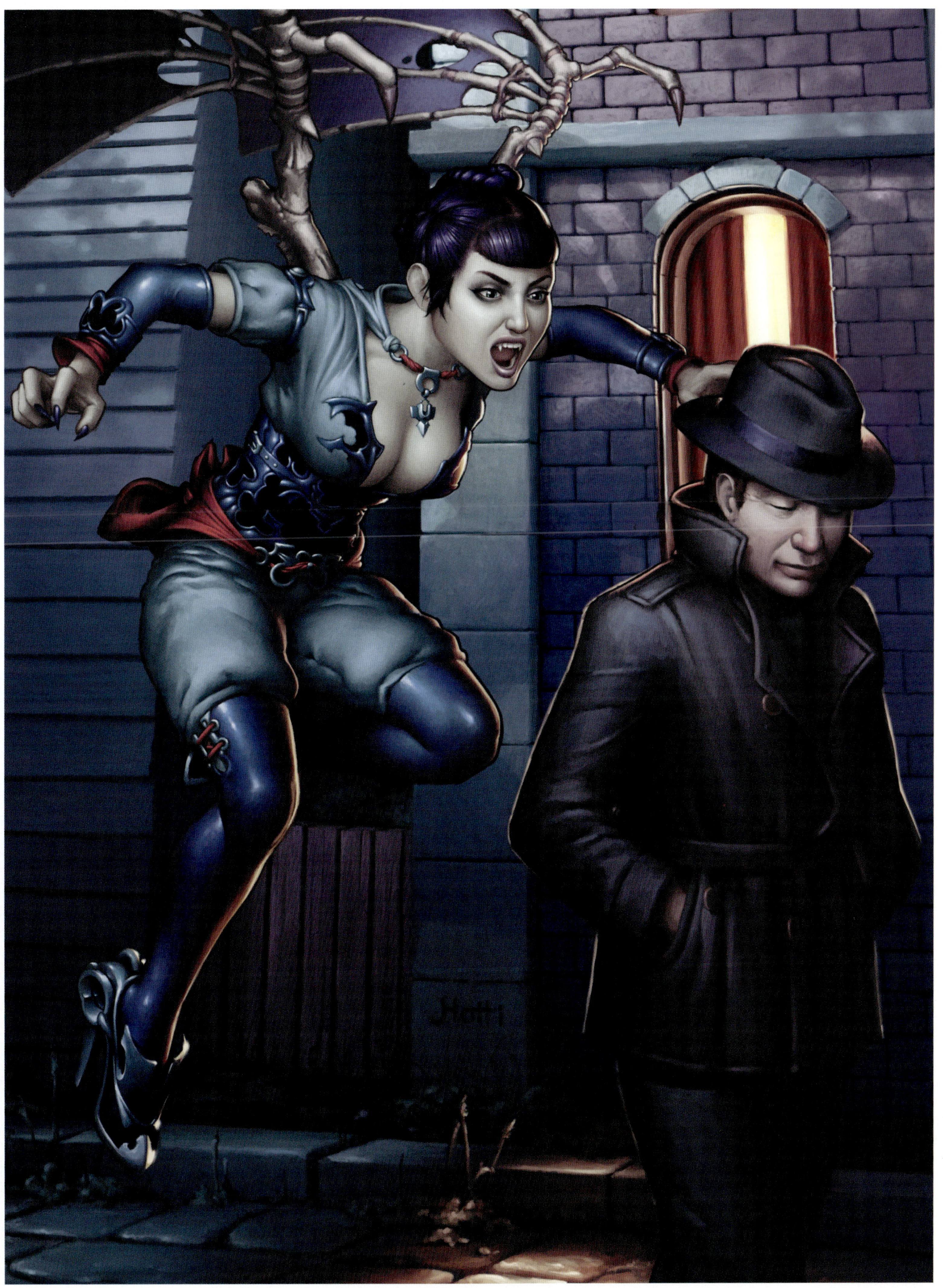

Late Night Snack

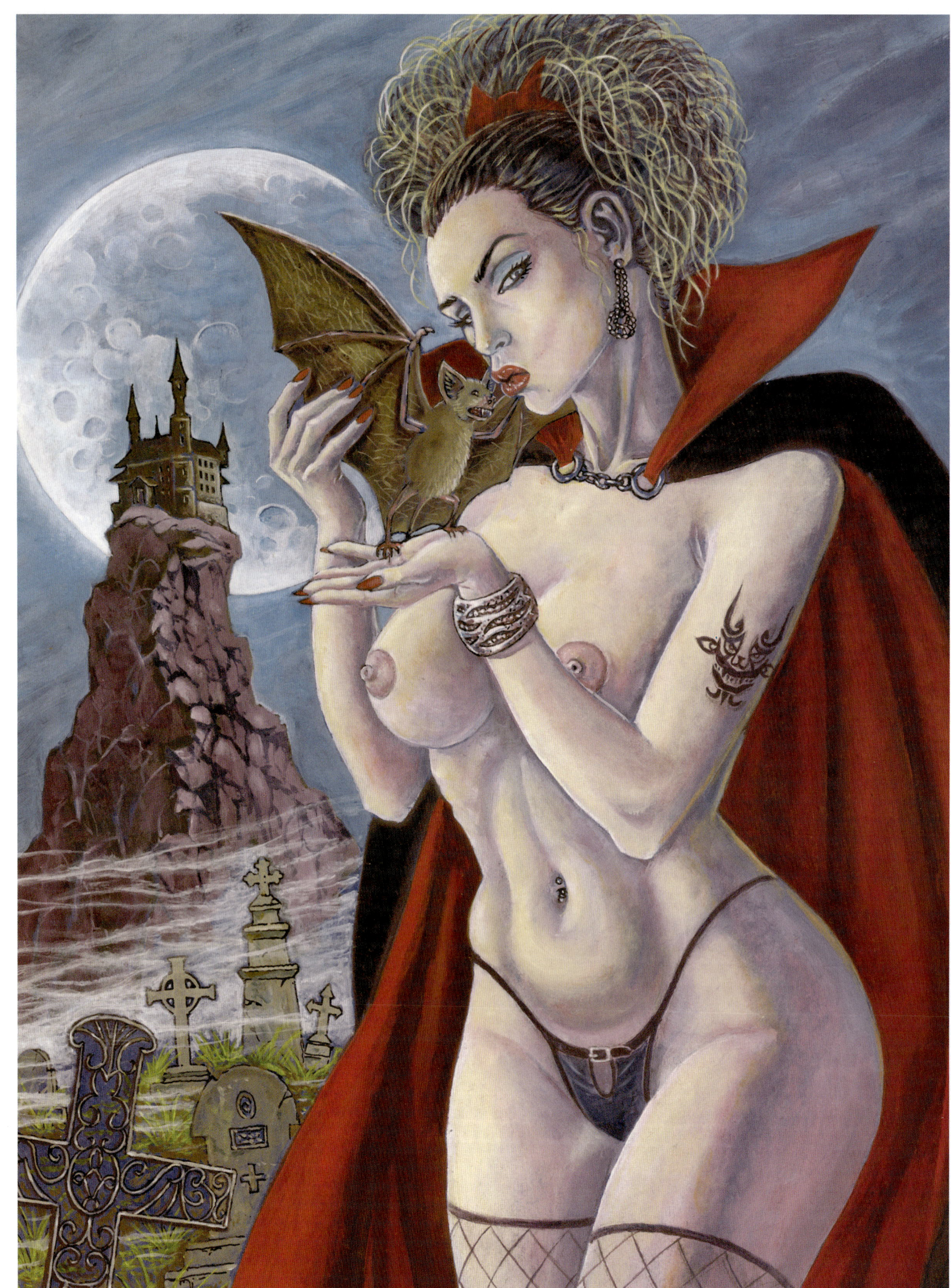

Mommy's Sweetest

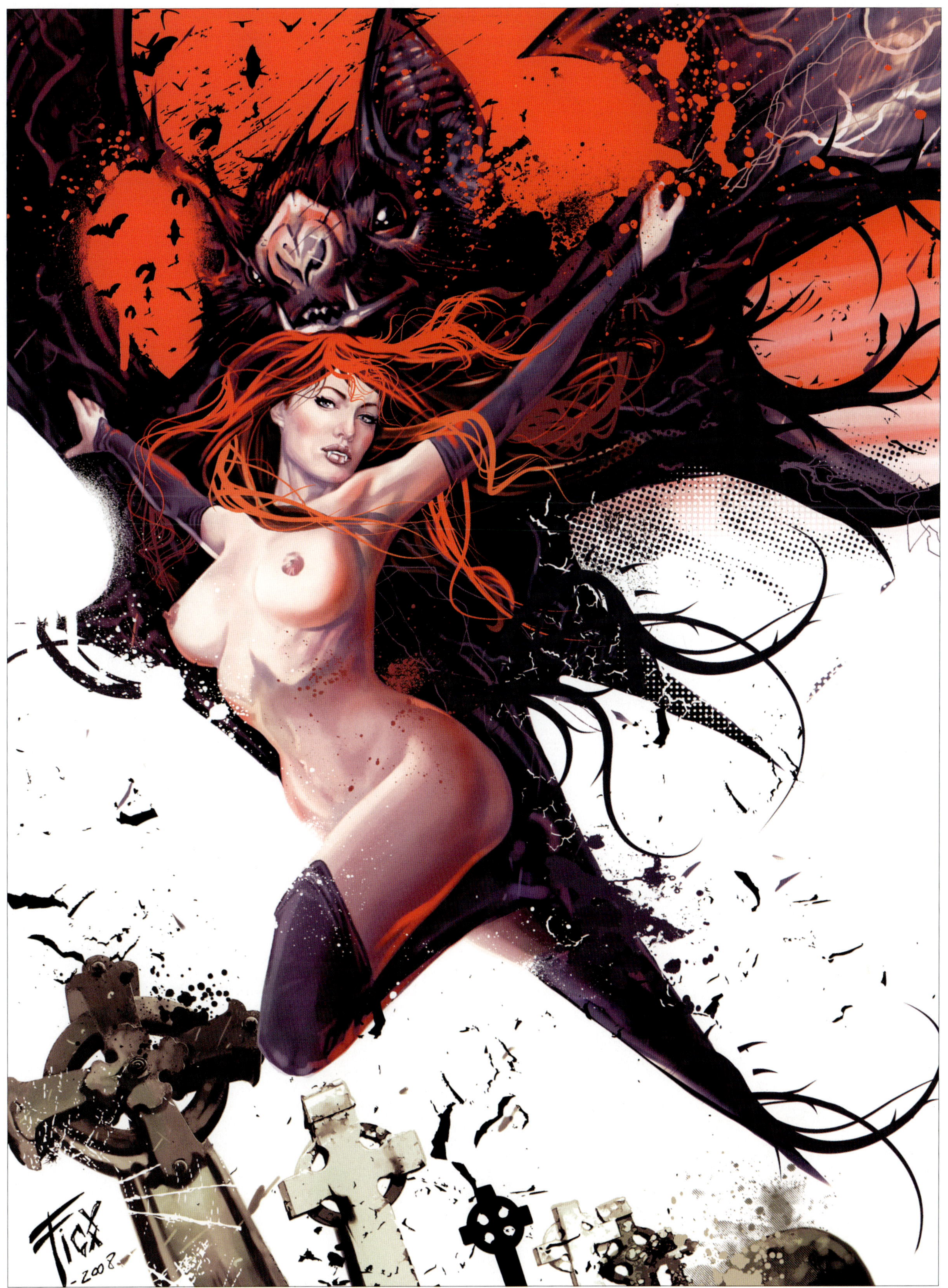

The Scent of Desire and Fear

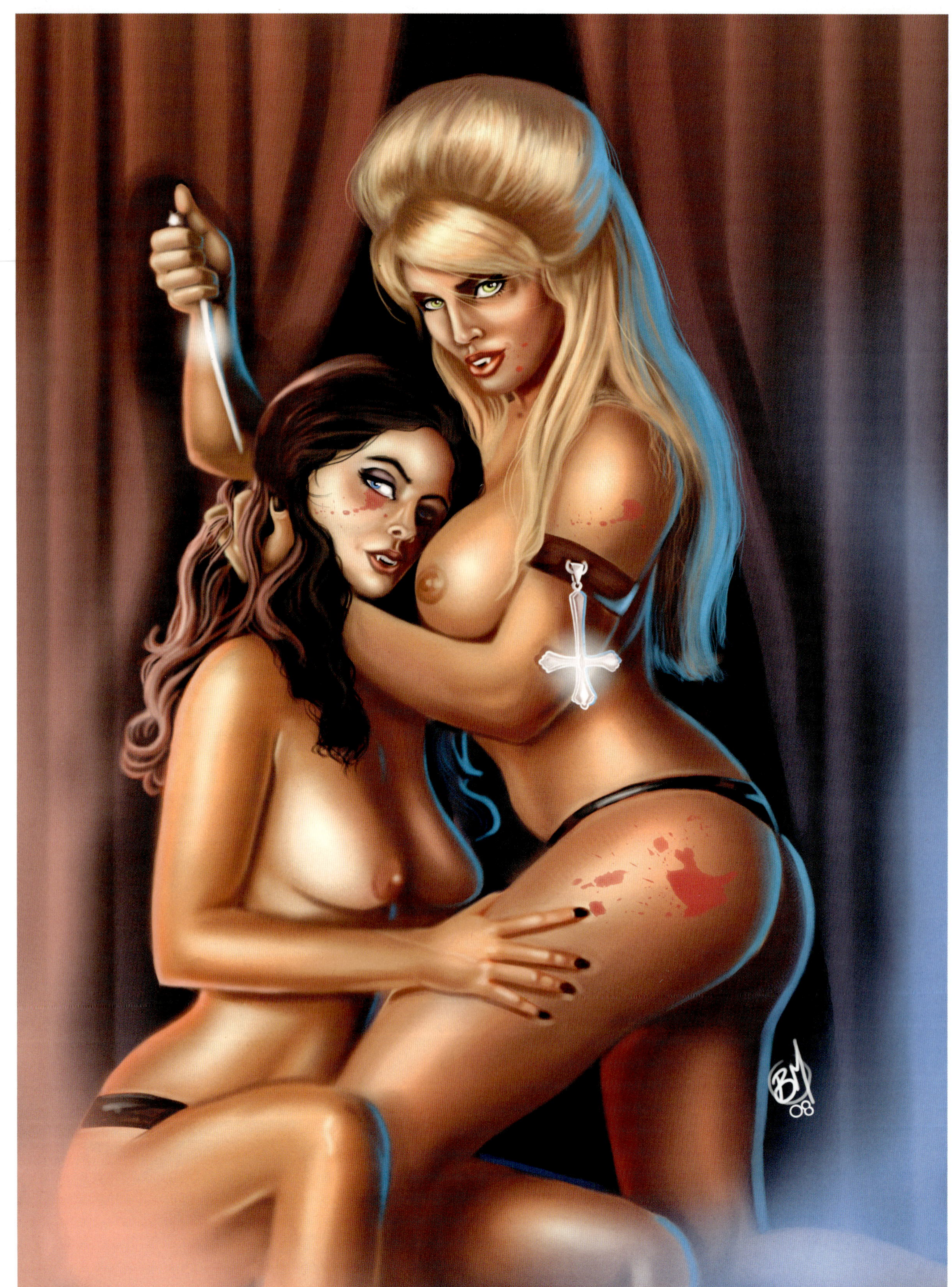

Trust is a Silver Dagger

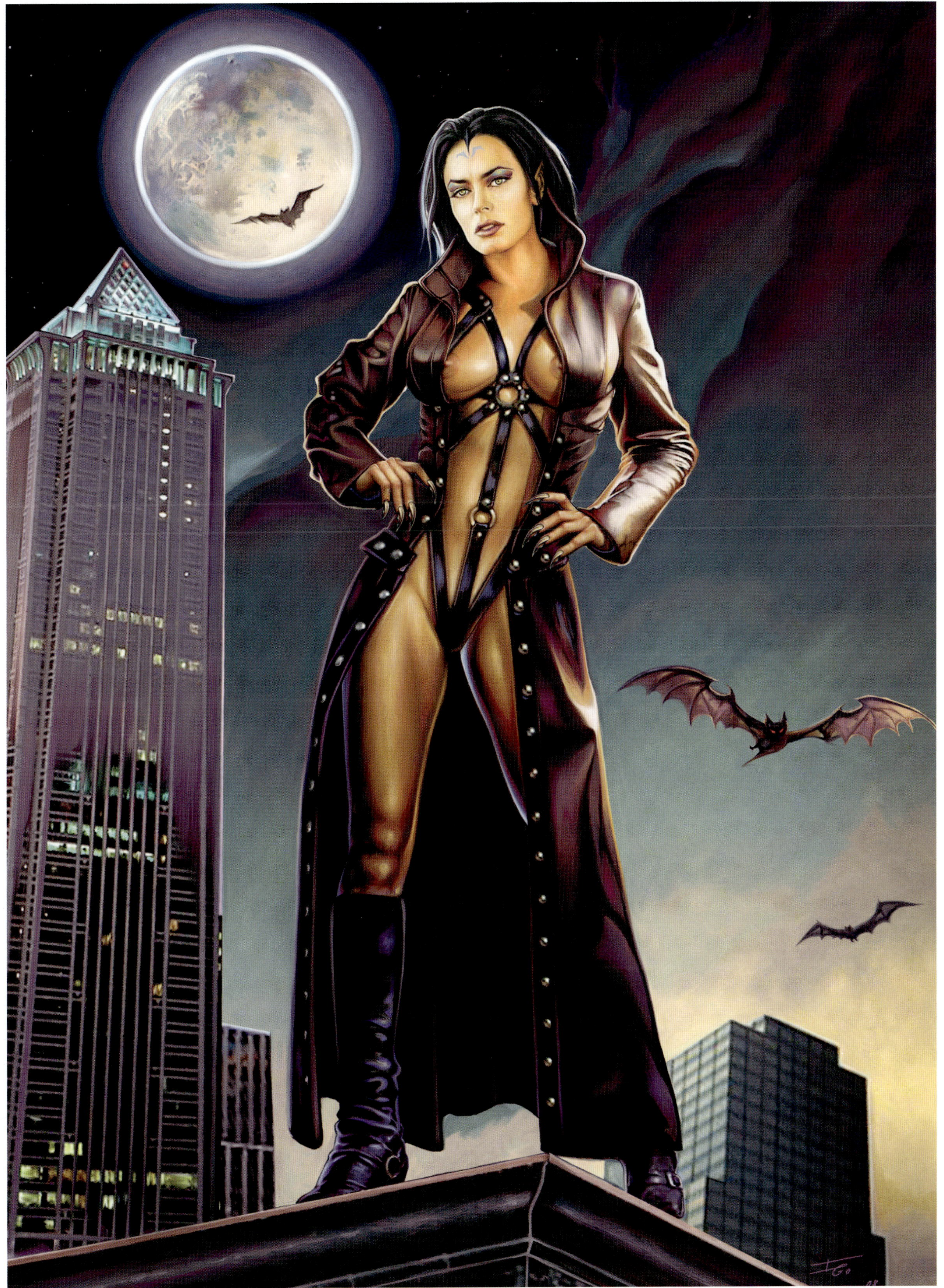

A Darker Fetish

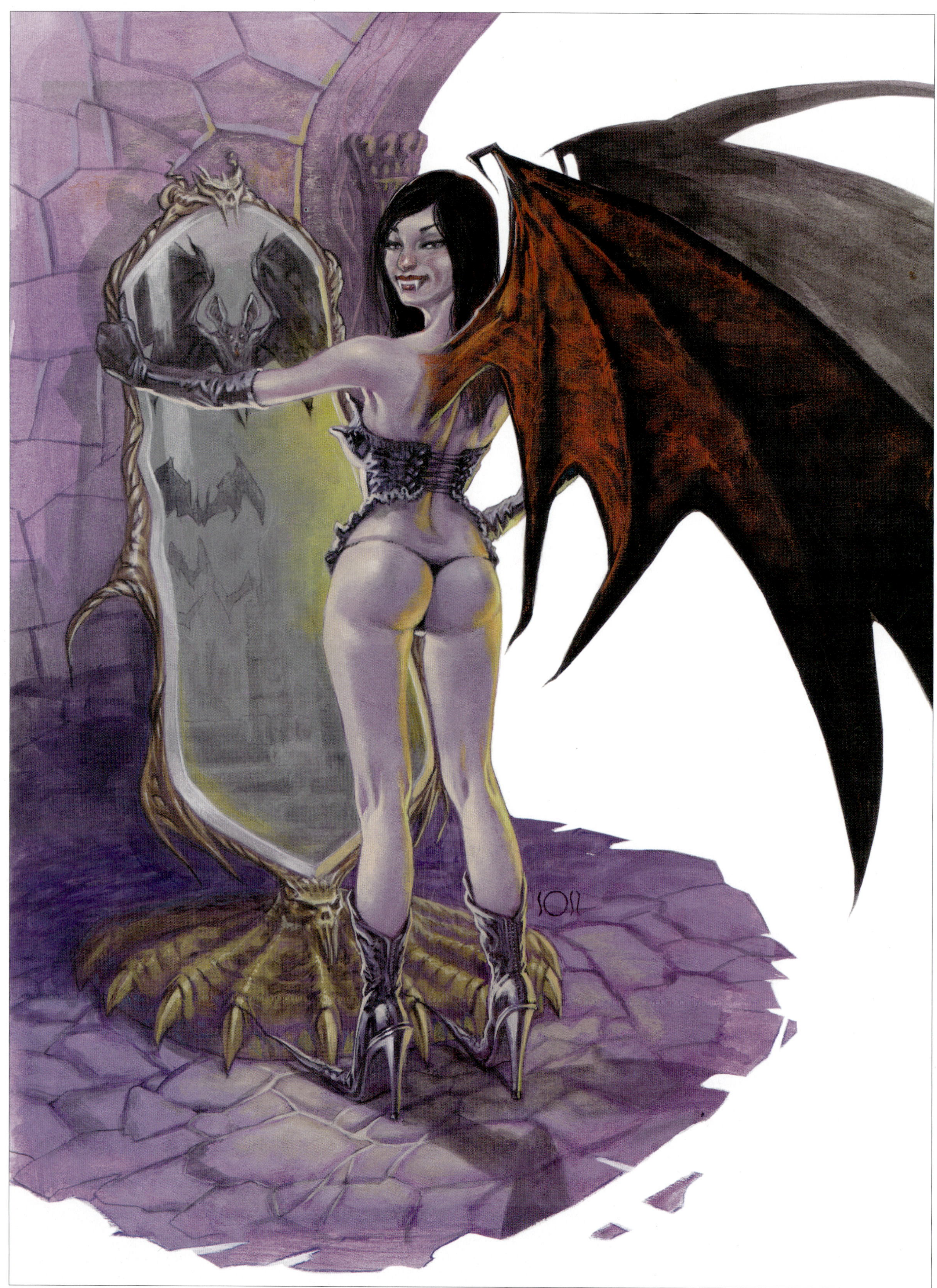

Mirrors Don't Lie

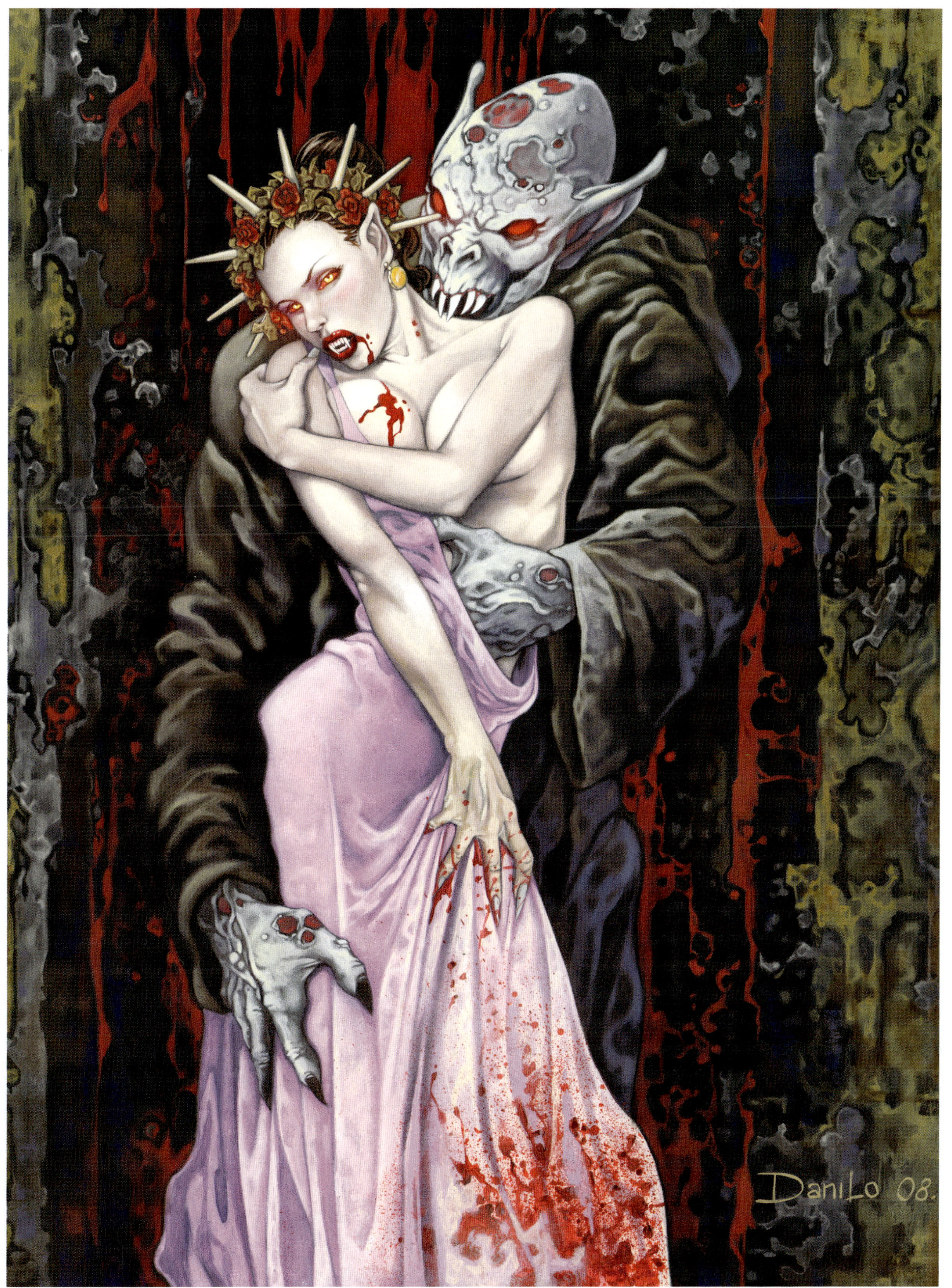

Crimson Wedding

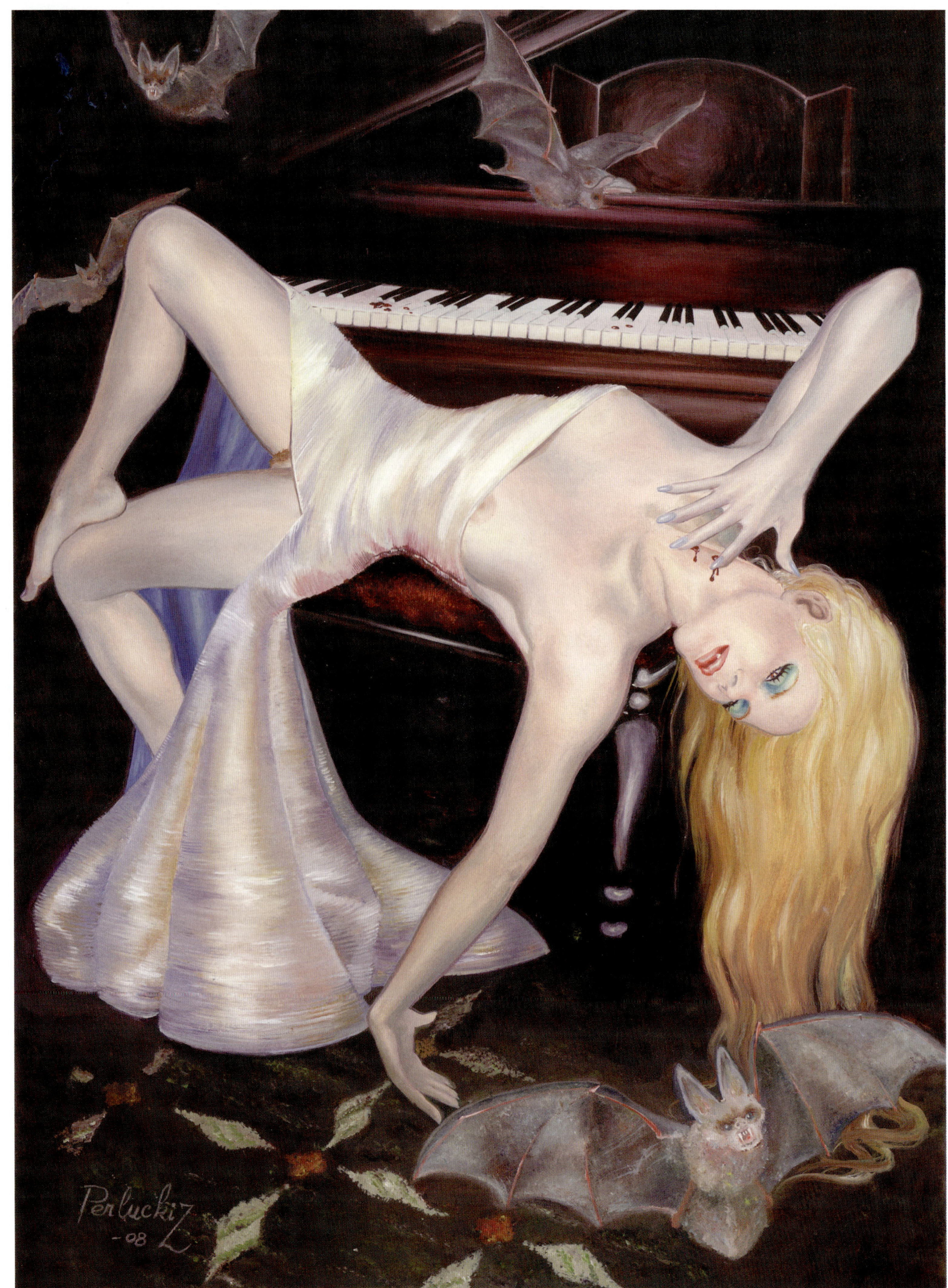

End Notes

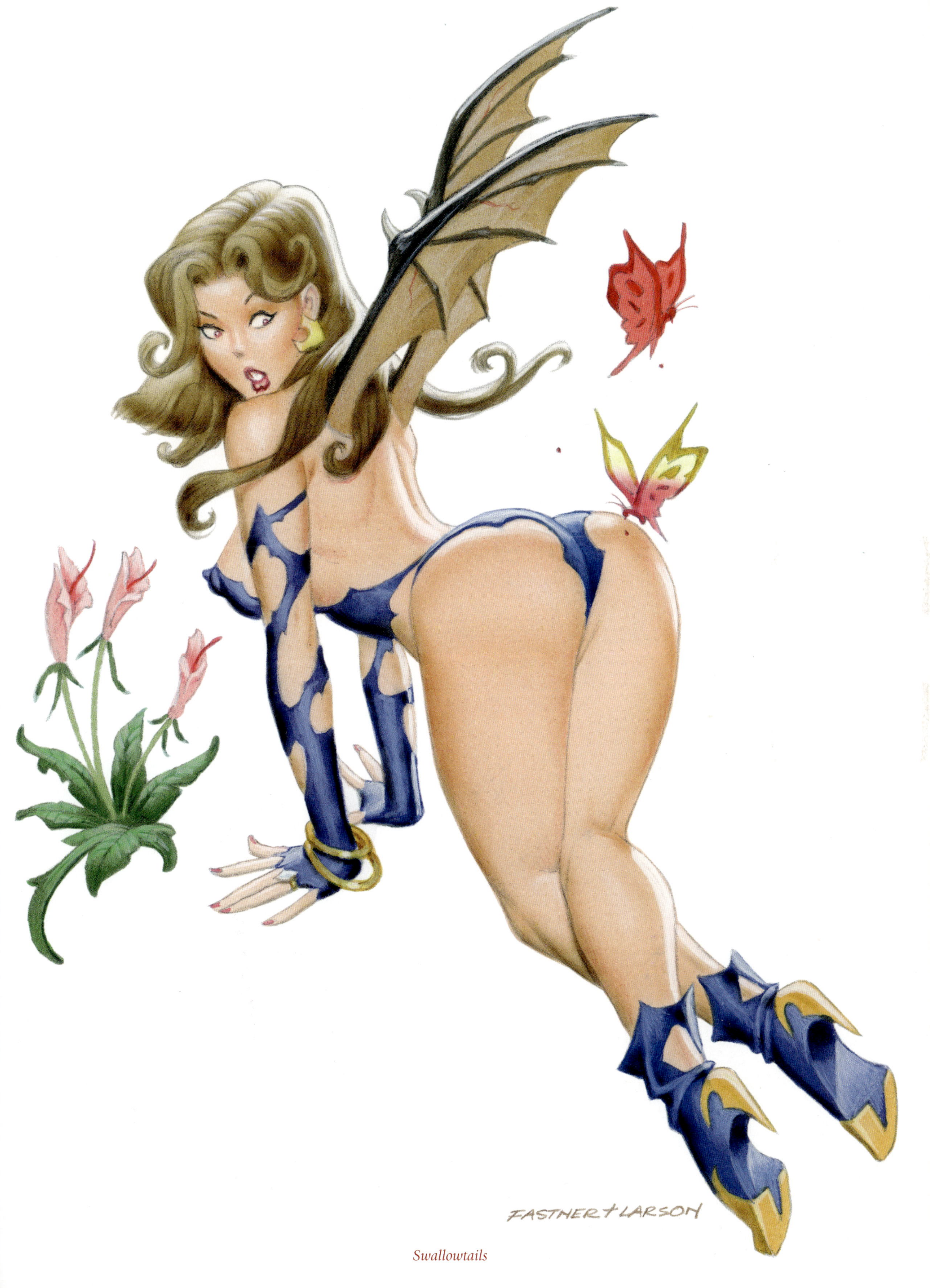

Swallowtails

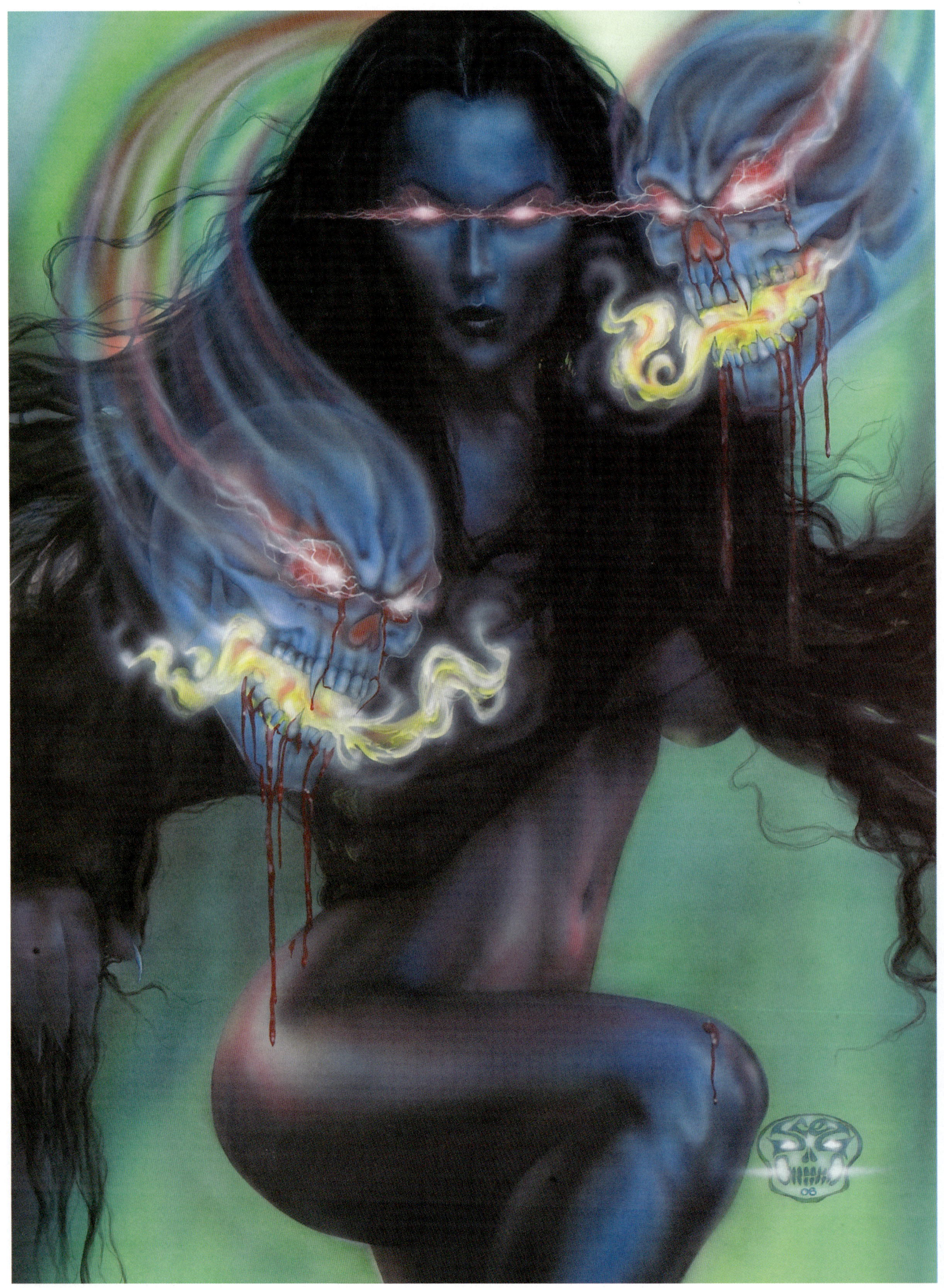

Essence of Damnation

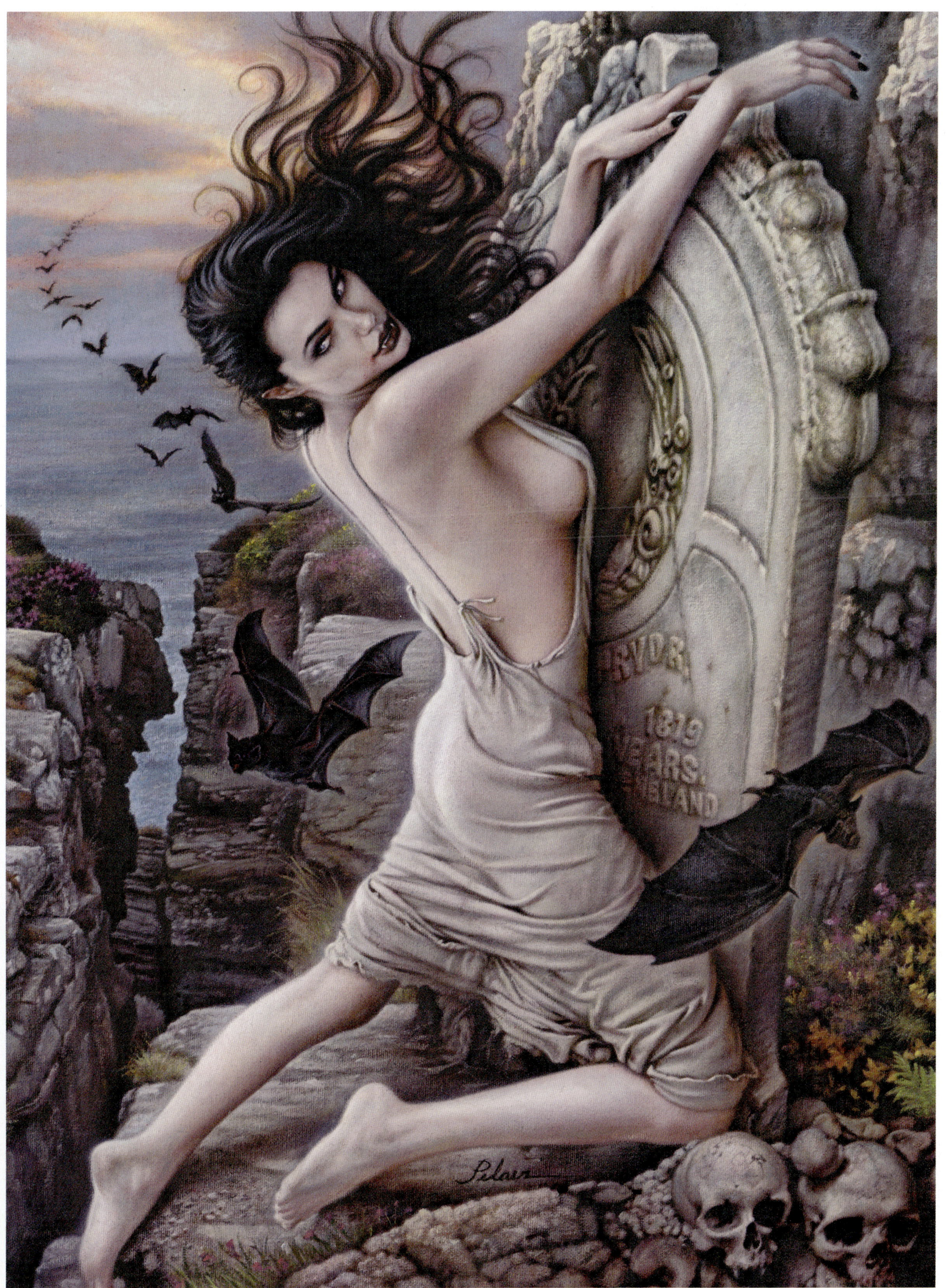

Her Resting Place

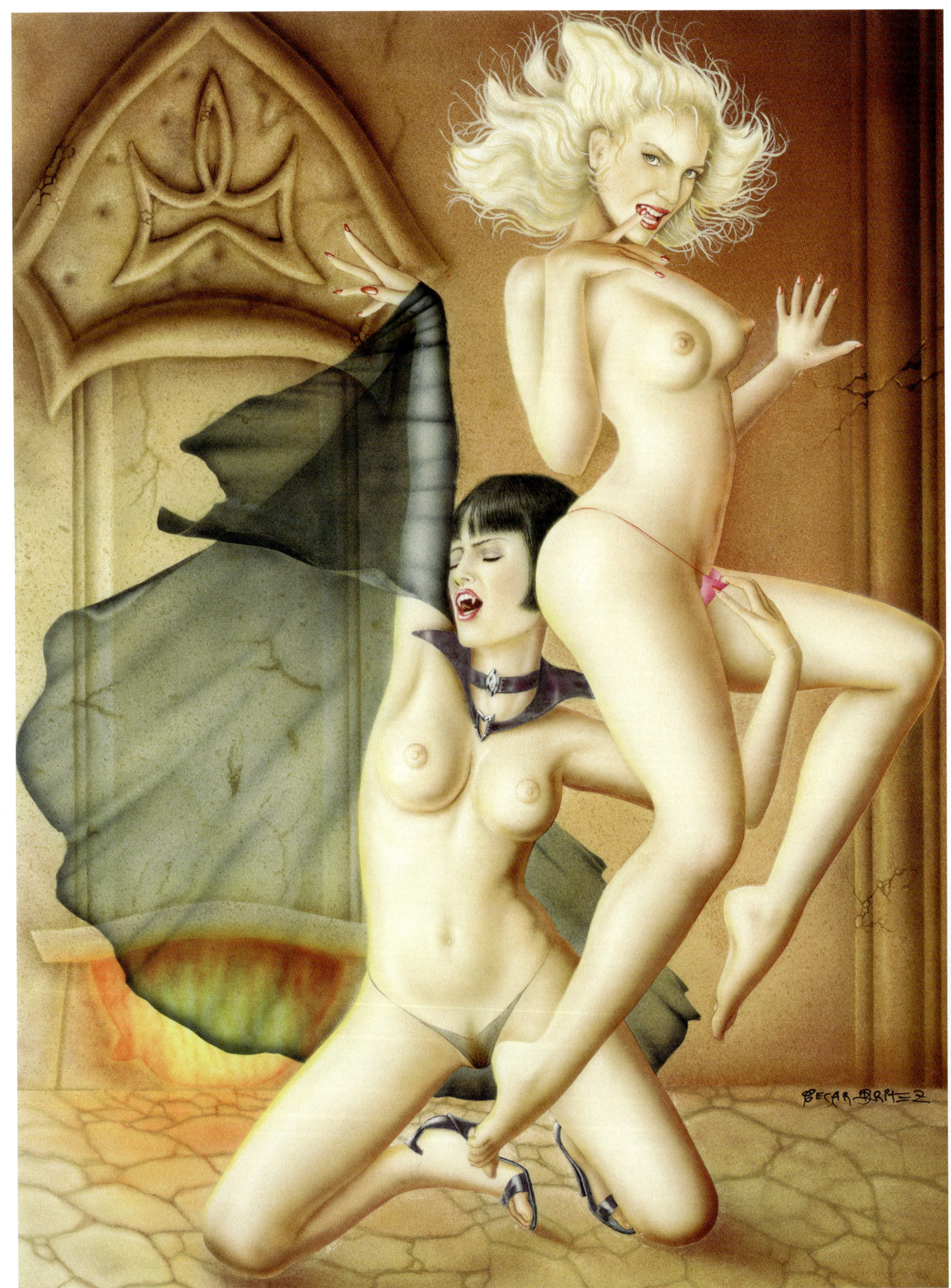

Eternally BFFs

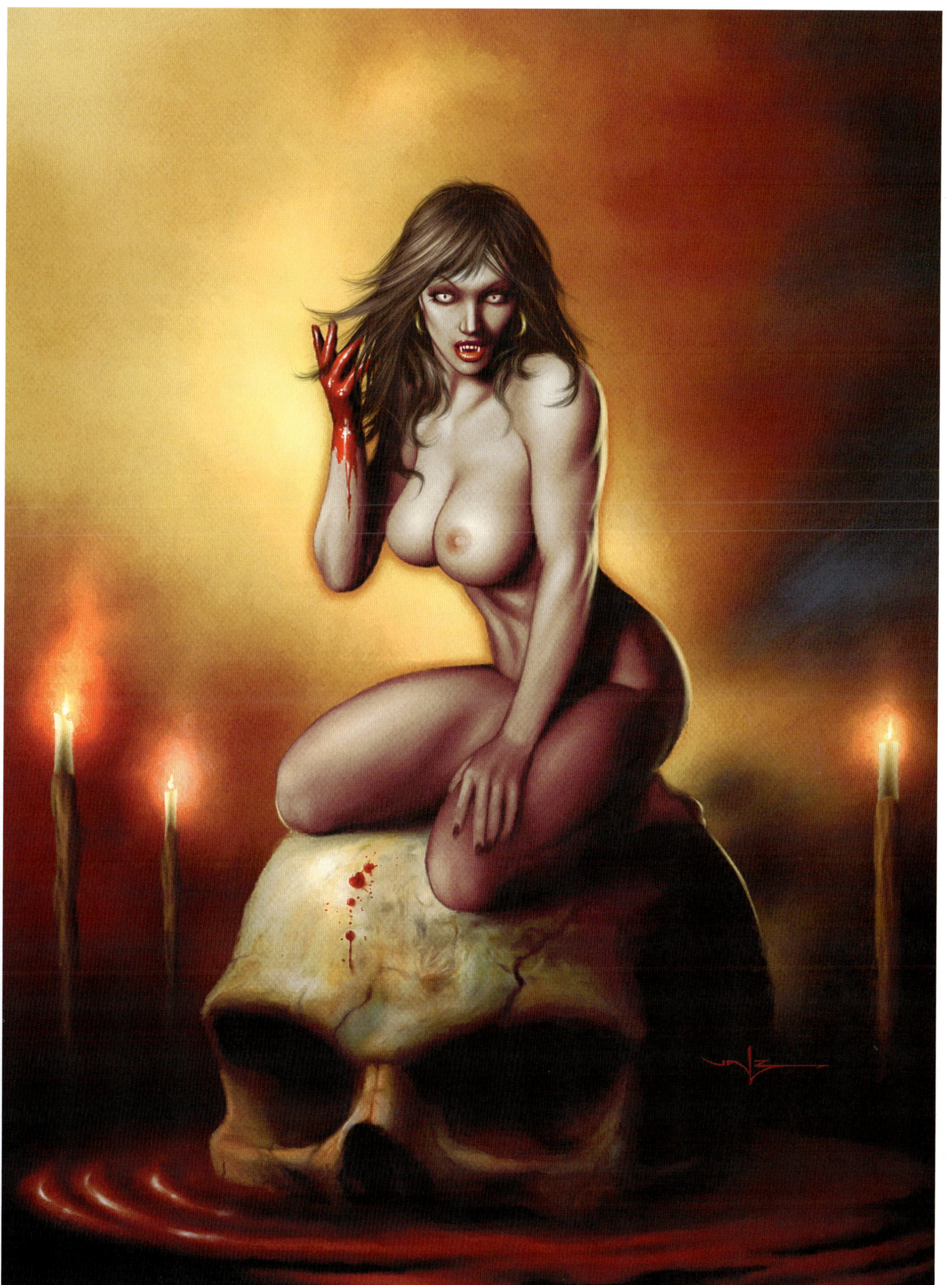

Floating on a Sea of Cruelty

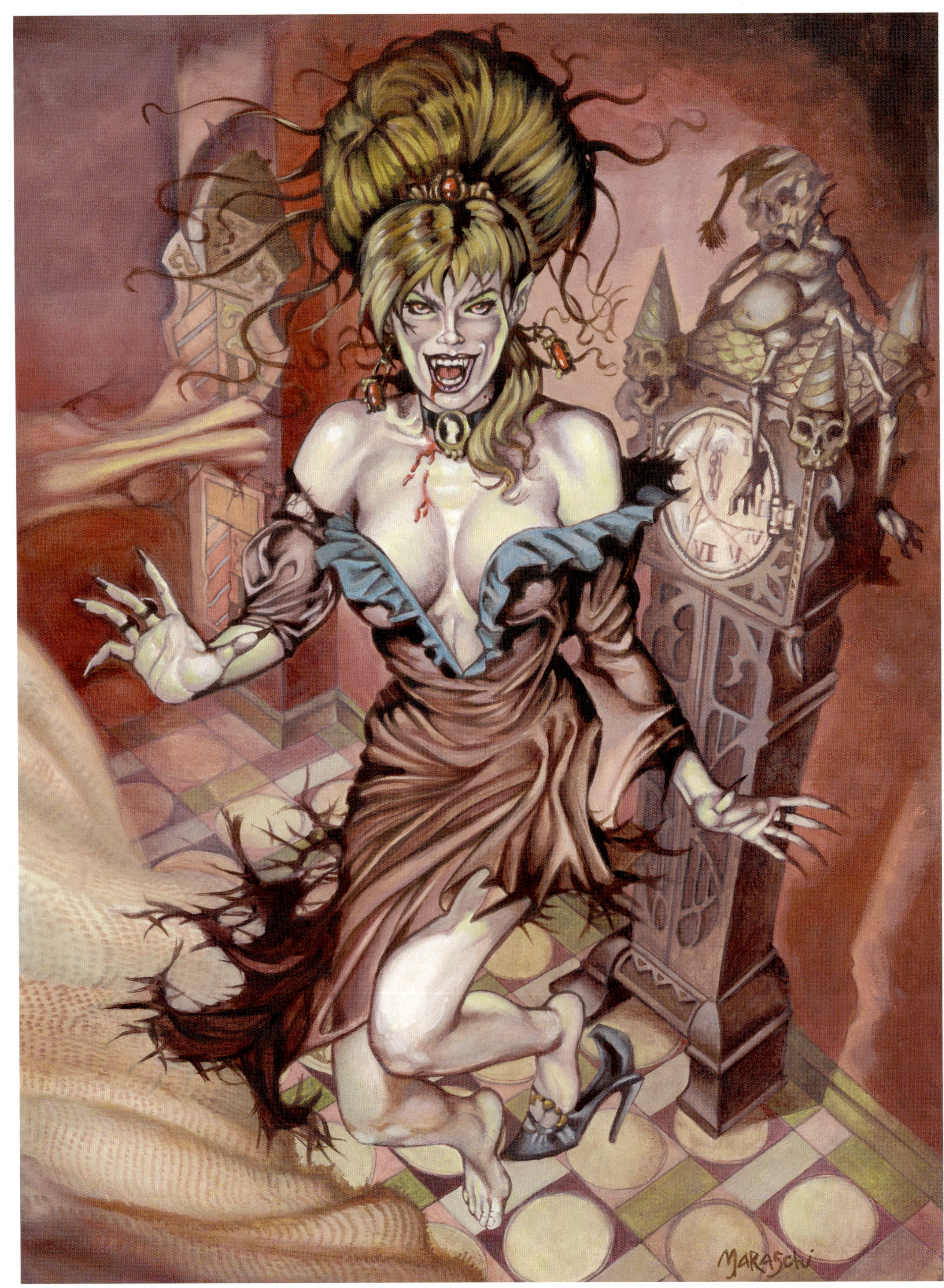

Midnight Madness

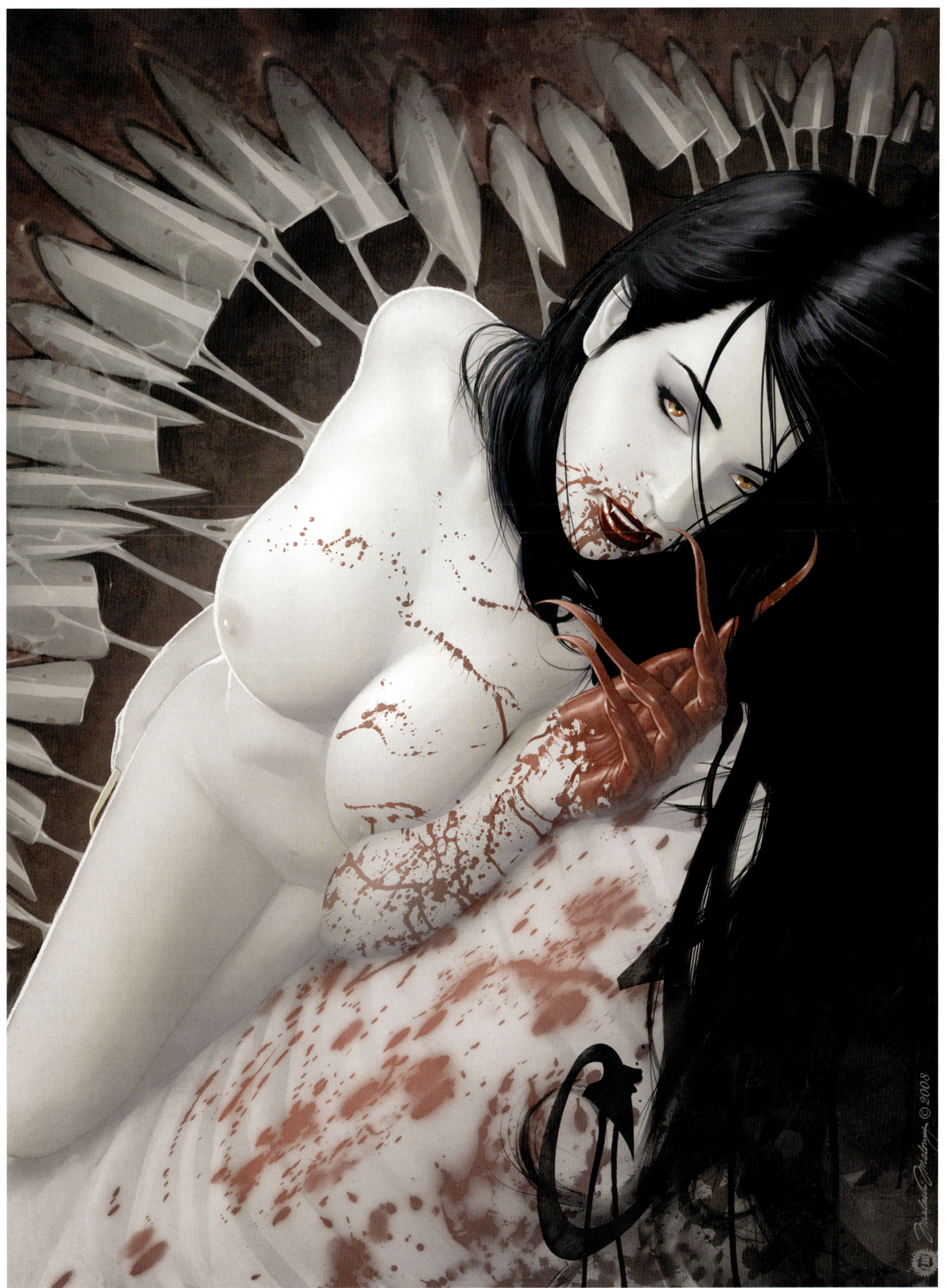

Drained but Satisfied

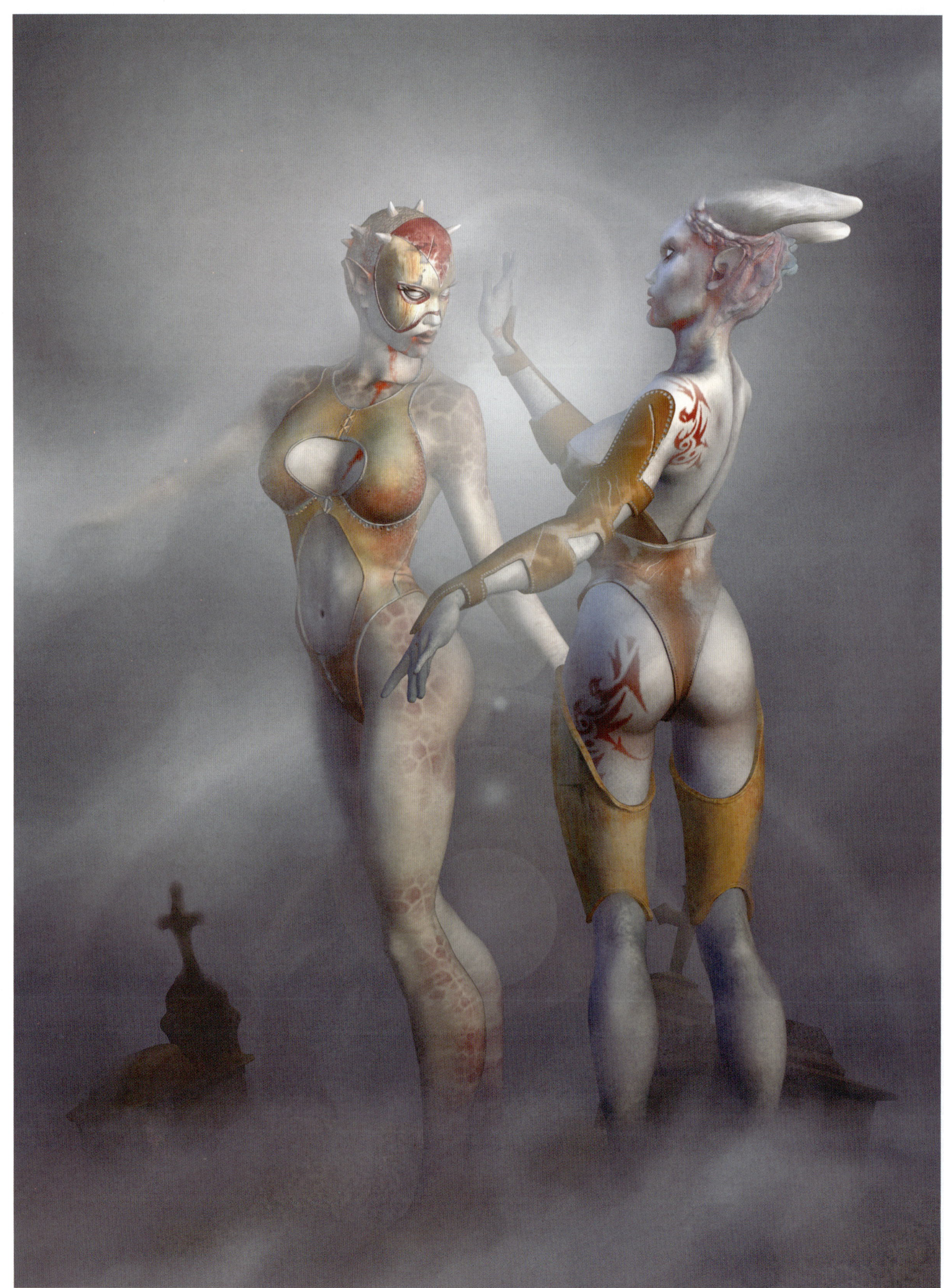

A Masquerade of Life

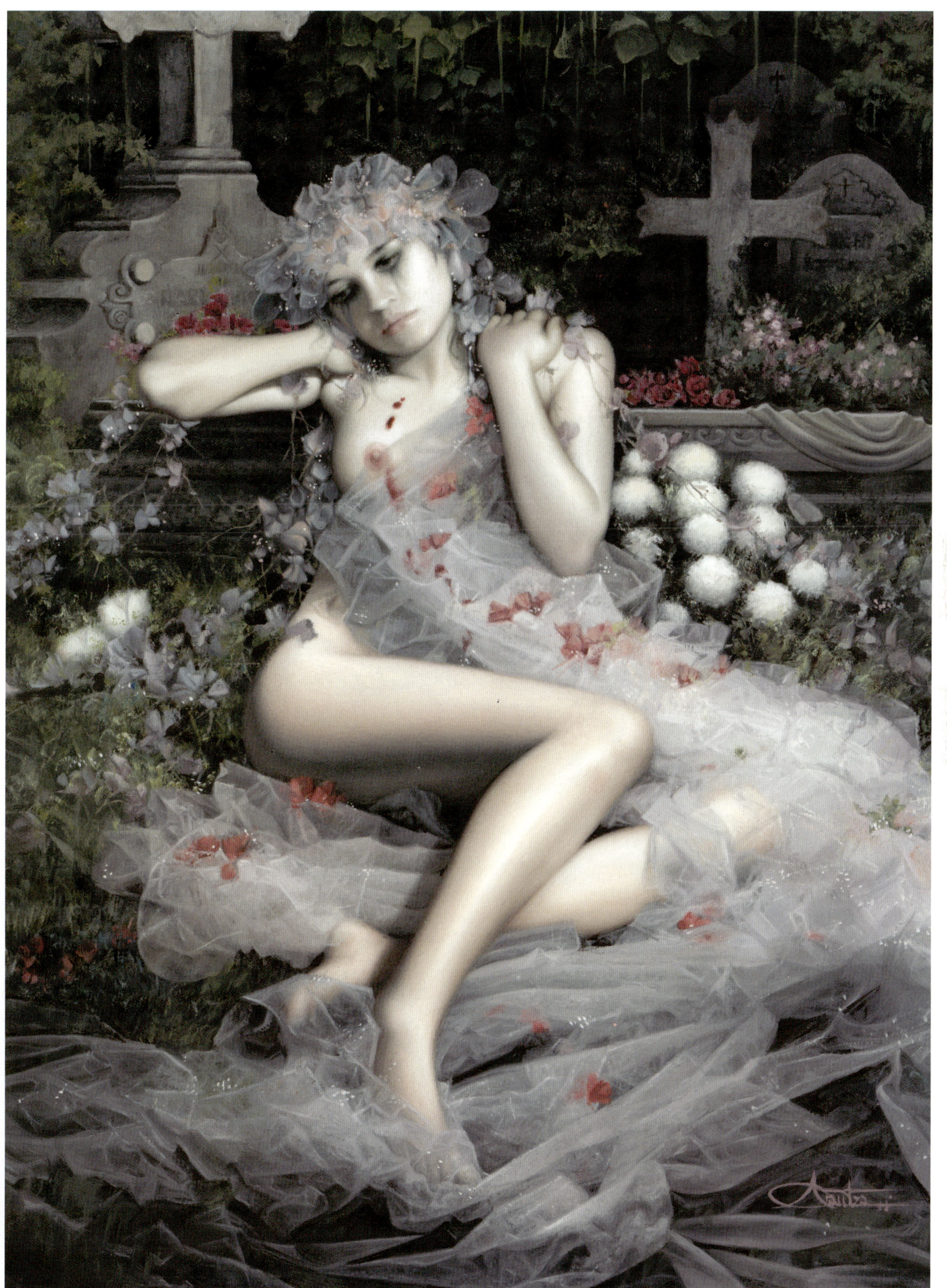

To What Might Have Been

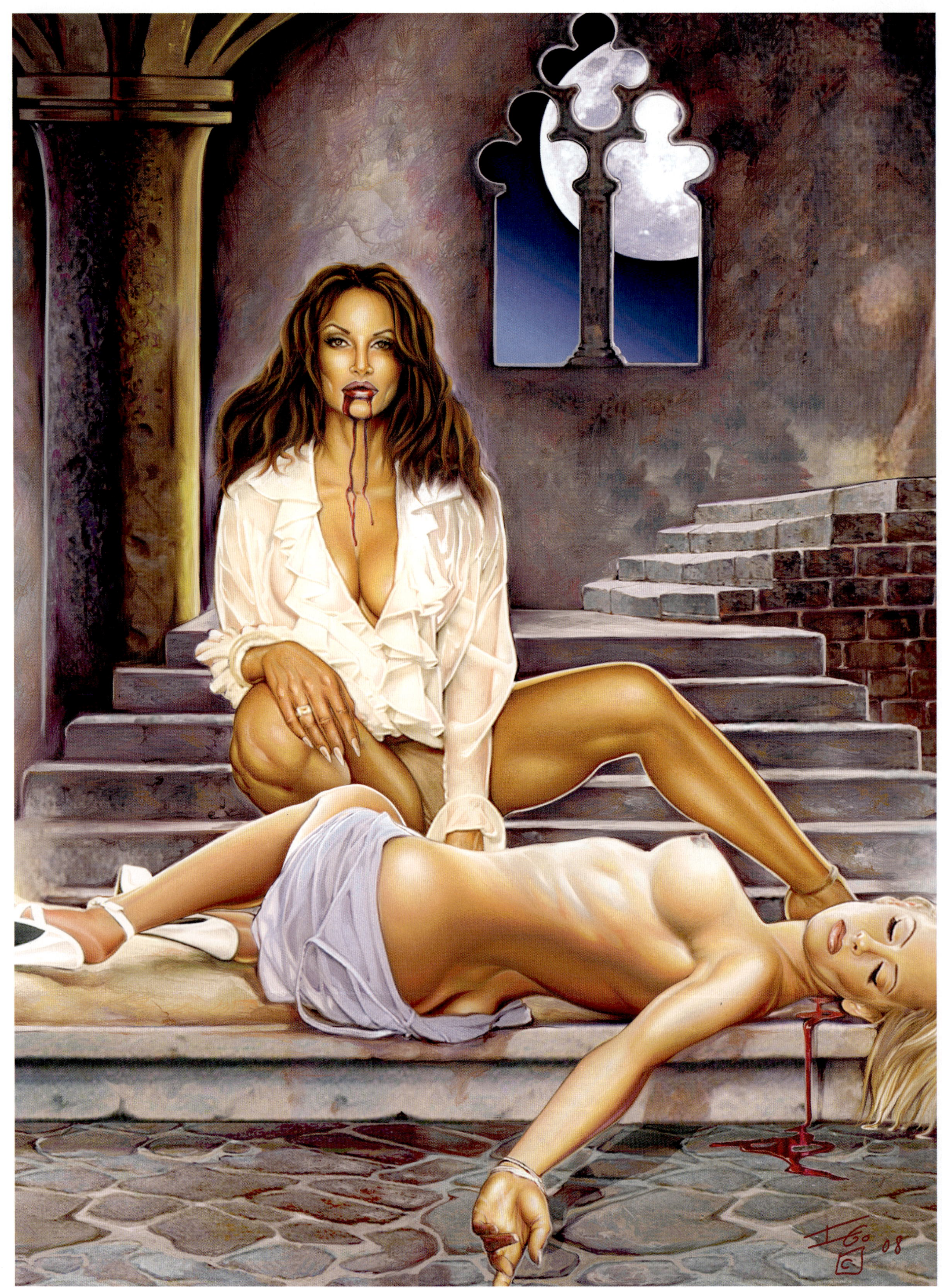

Her Beauty Secret - Finally Revealed

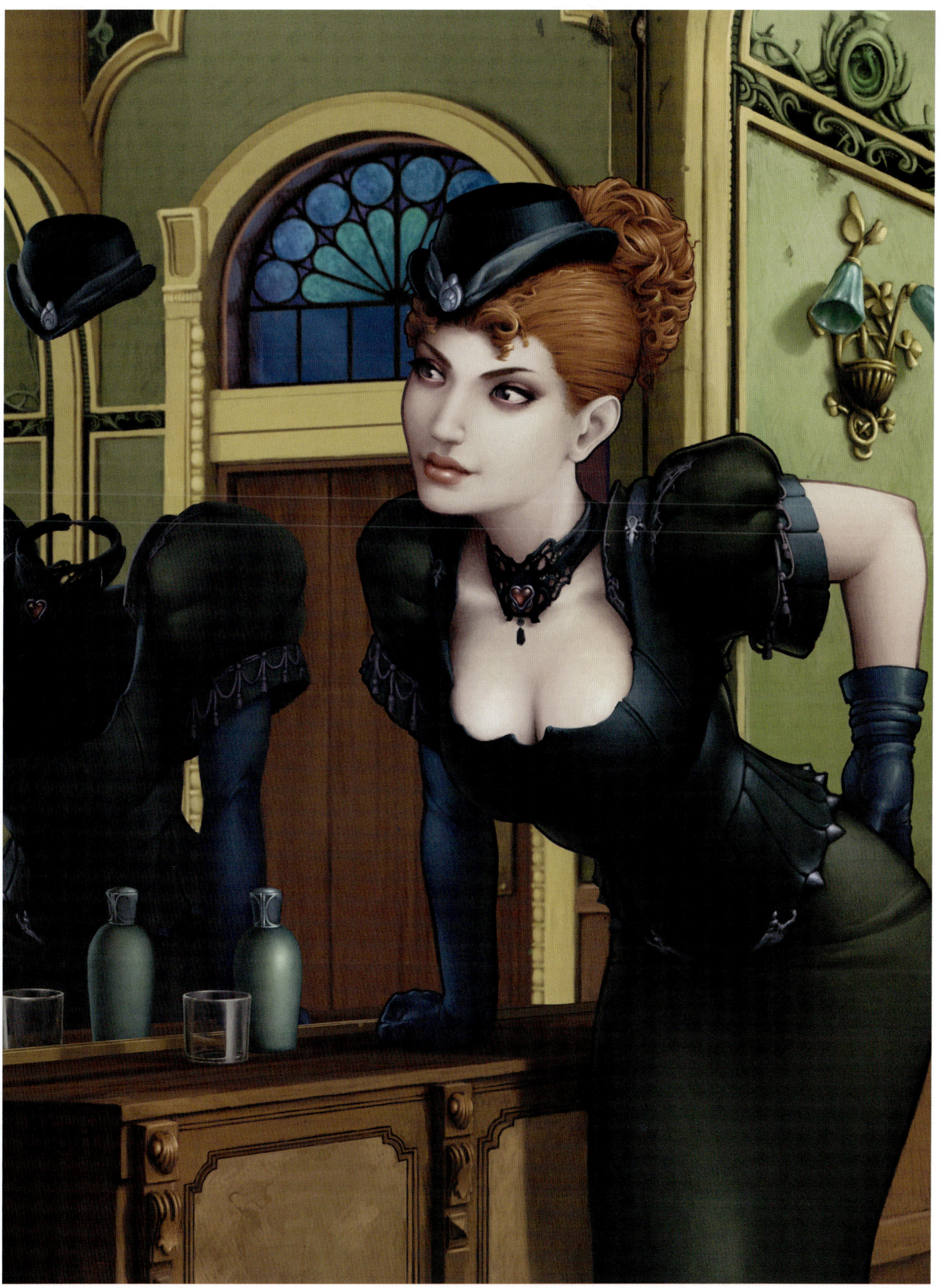

"Seriously...how do I look?"

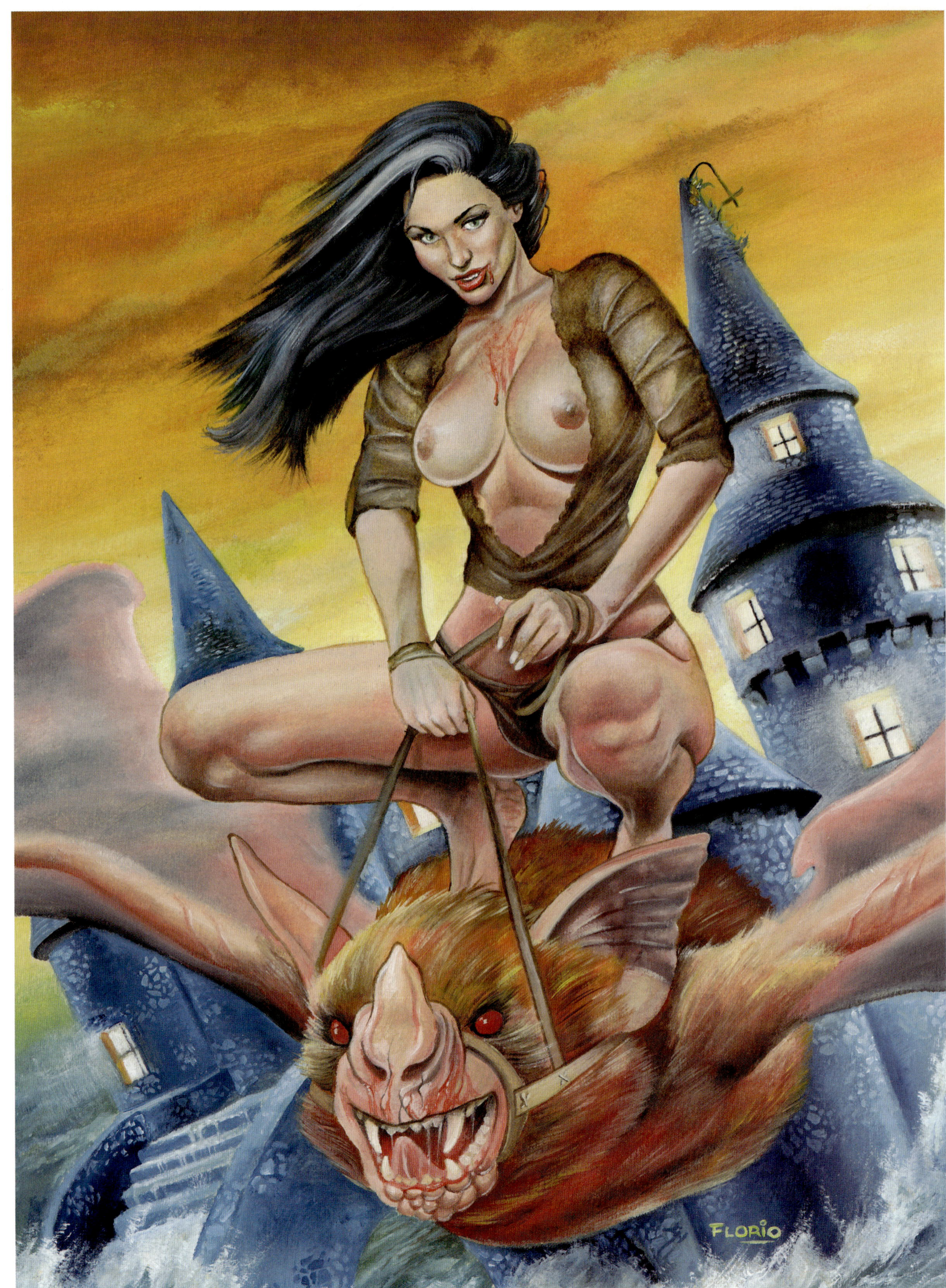

Joy Ride

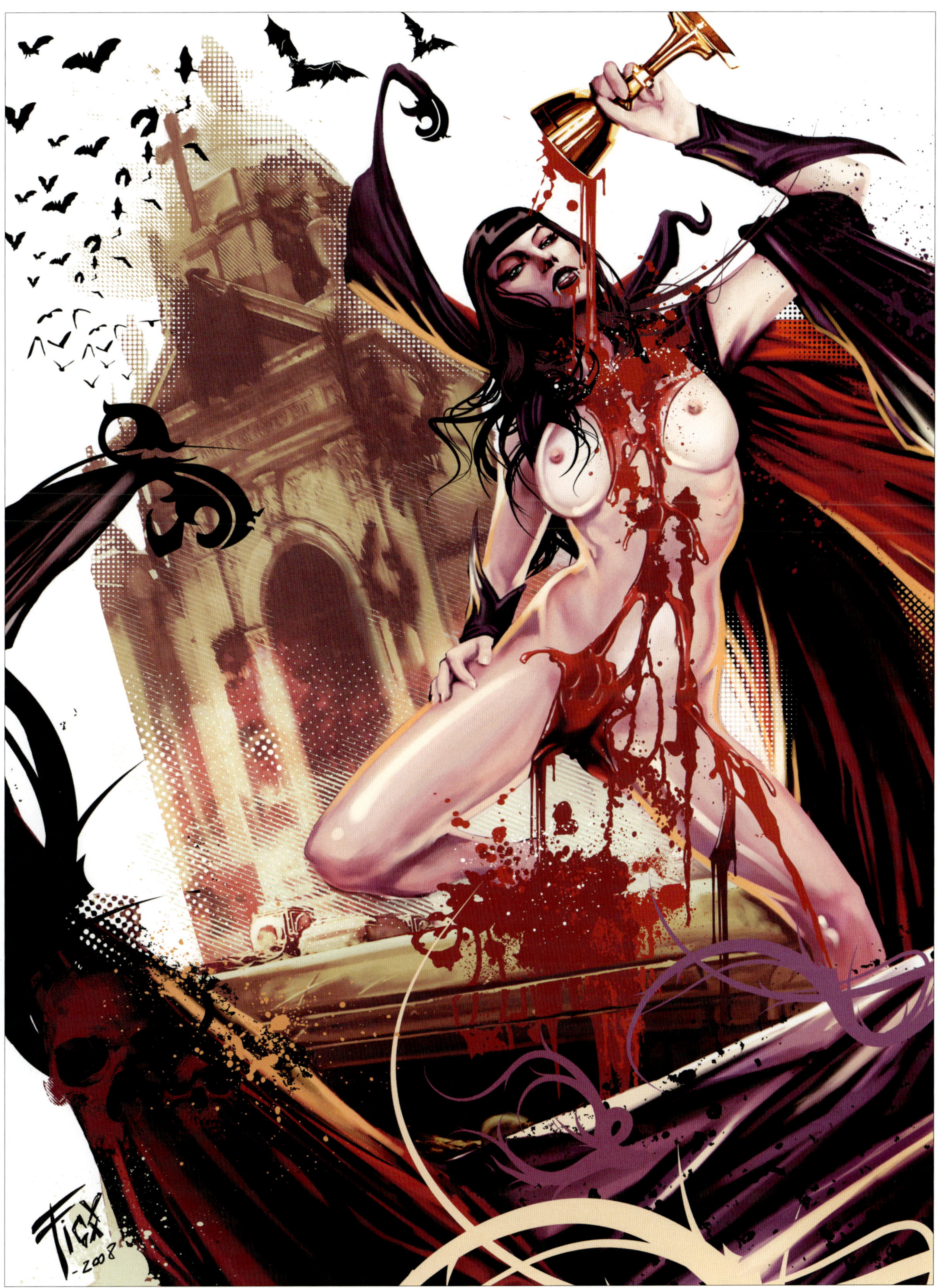

To Insult the Maker - Life Eternal for Her Soul

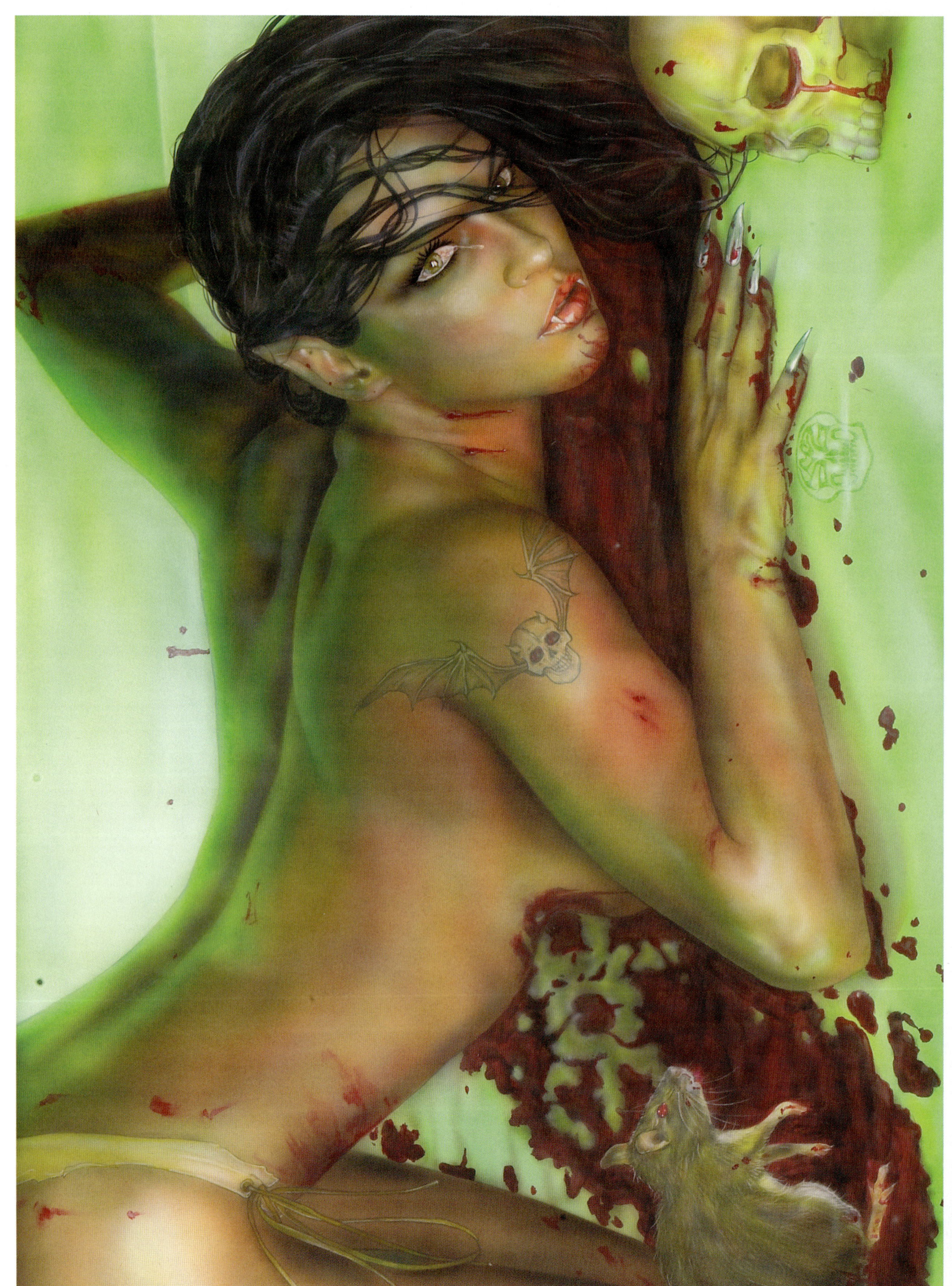

Bleed for Mercy

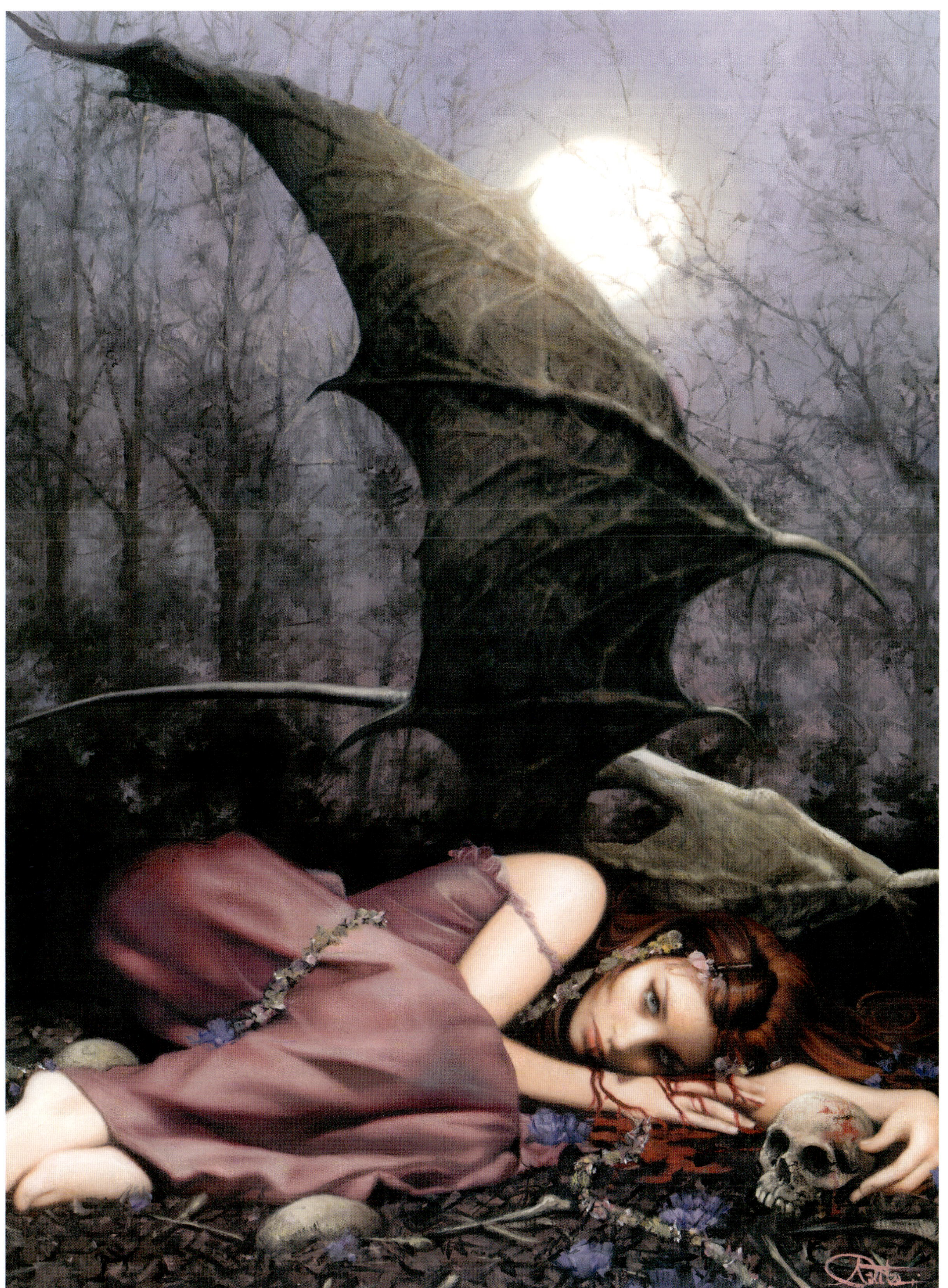

Cold Comfort

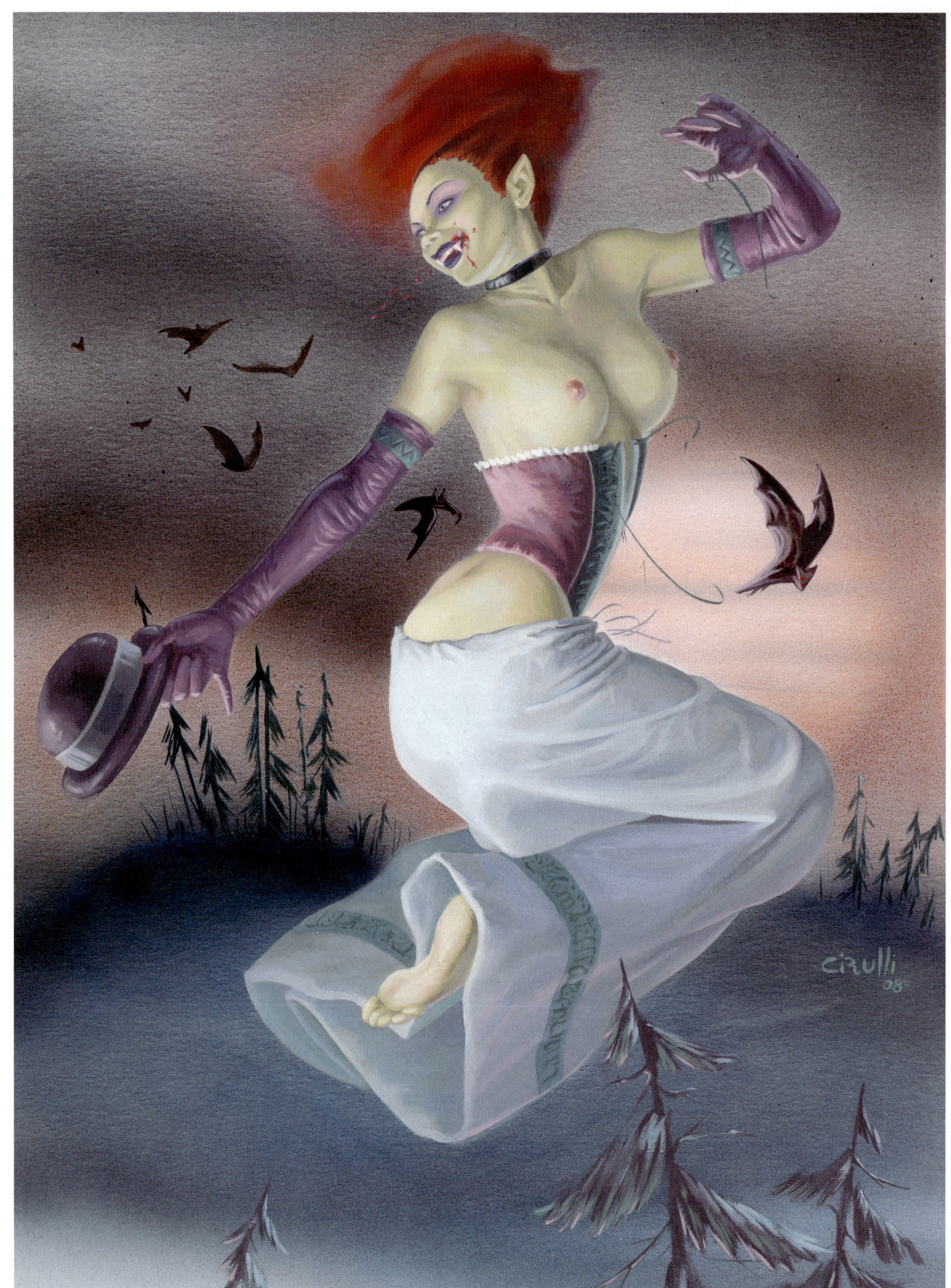

Caution to the Wind

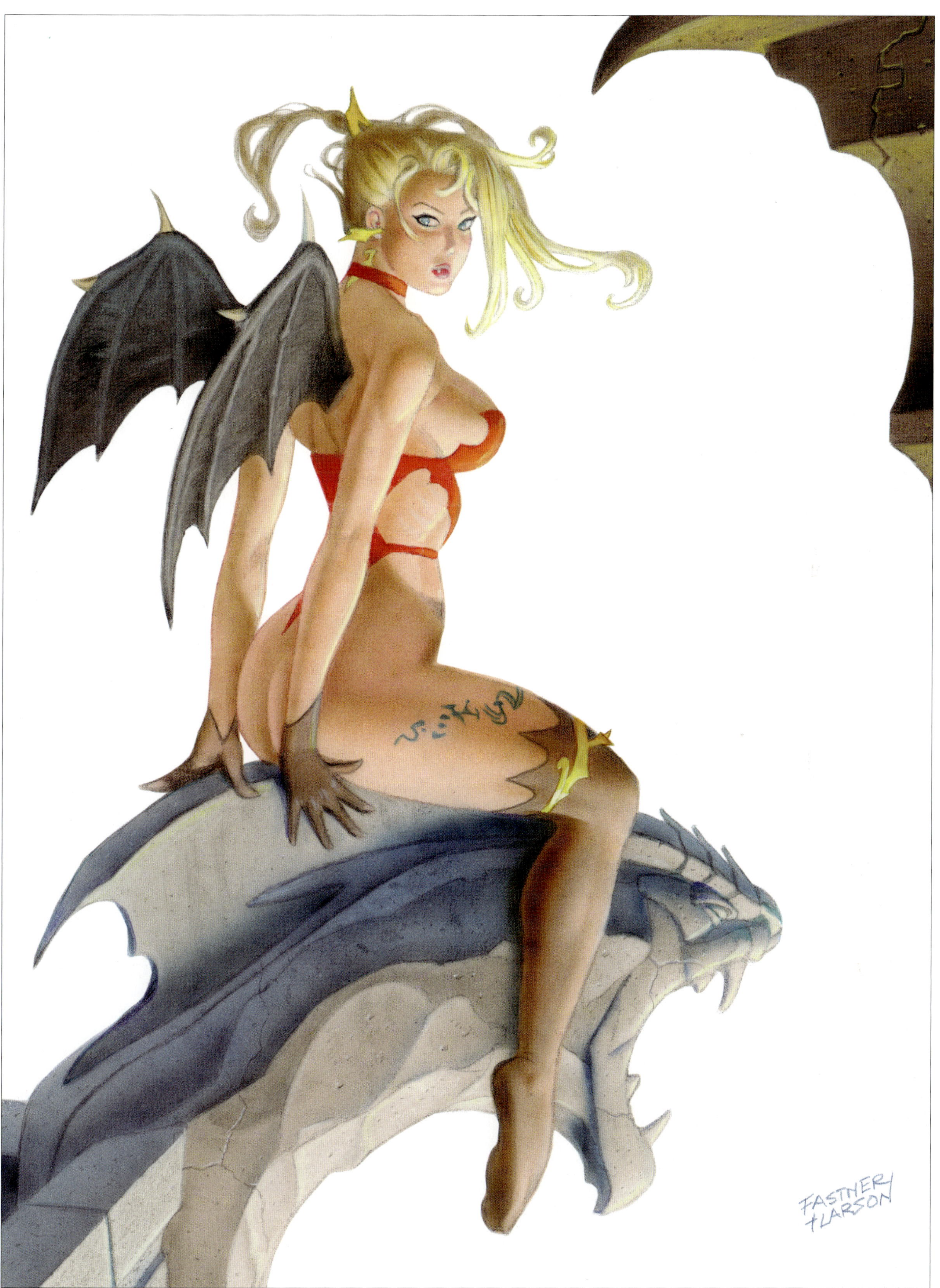

The Lookout

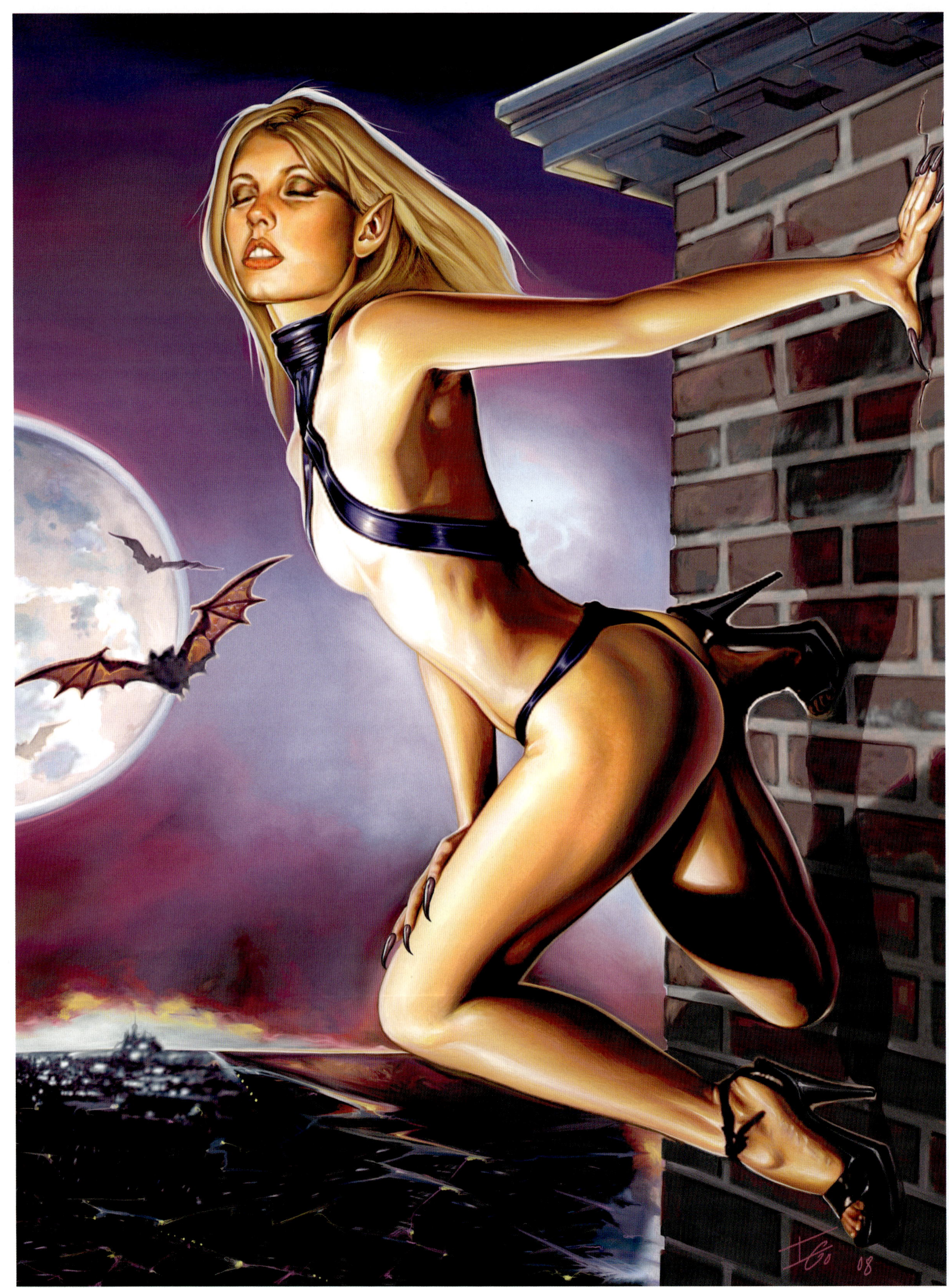

Night Air Chill

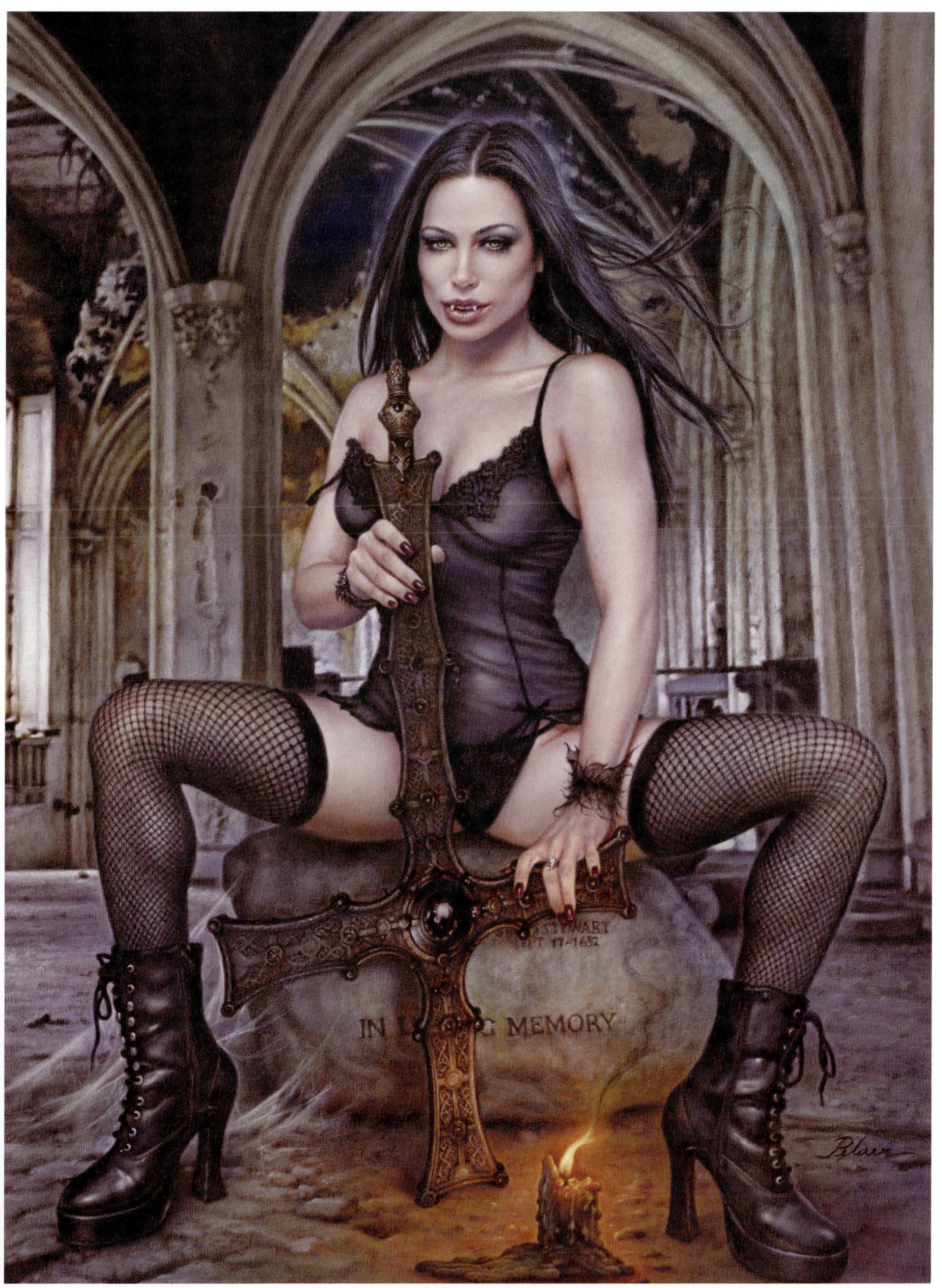

In Loving Memory

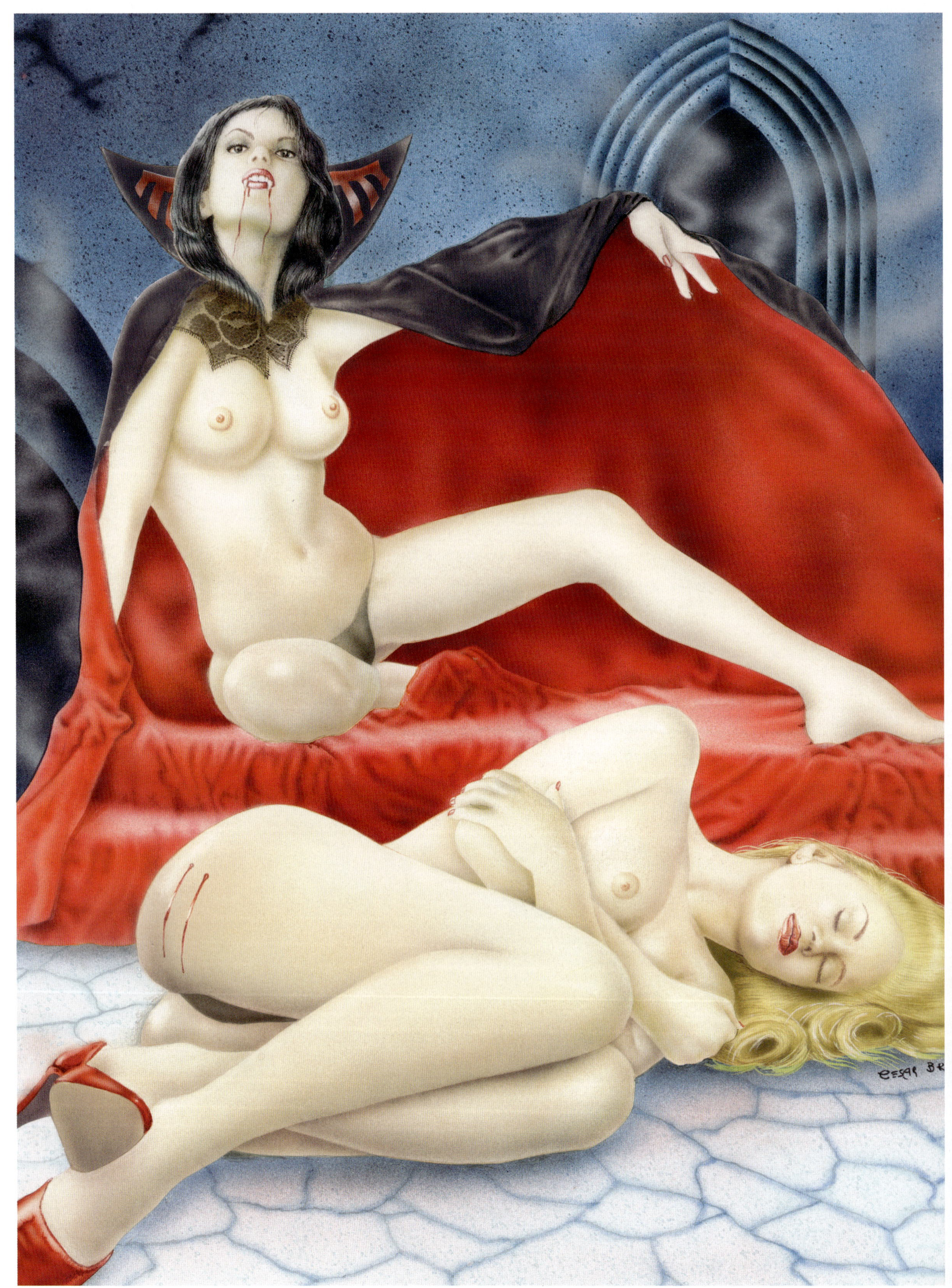

A Little Variety

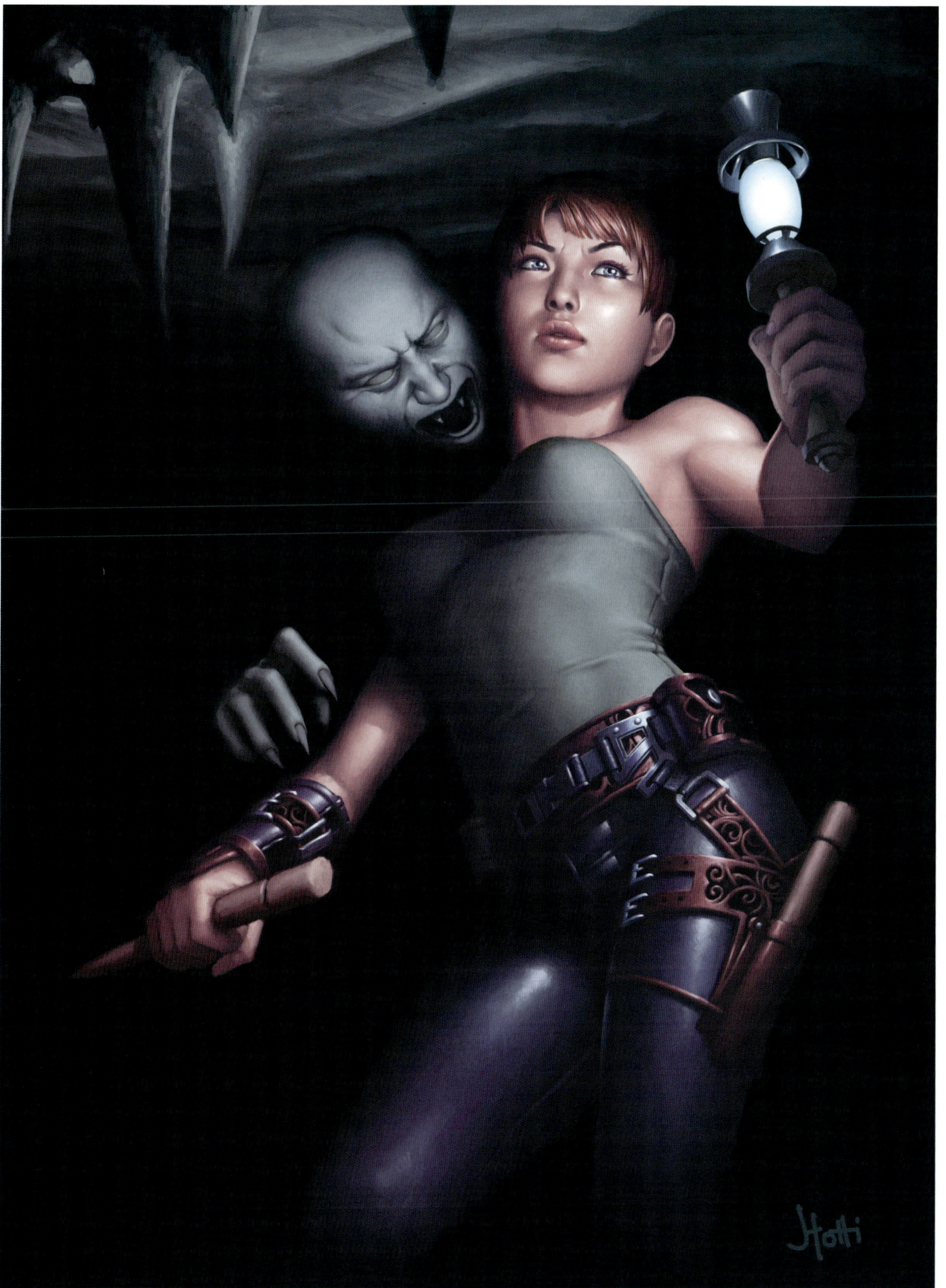

Prey

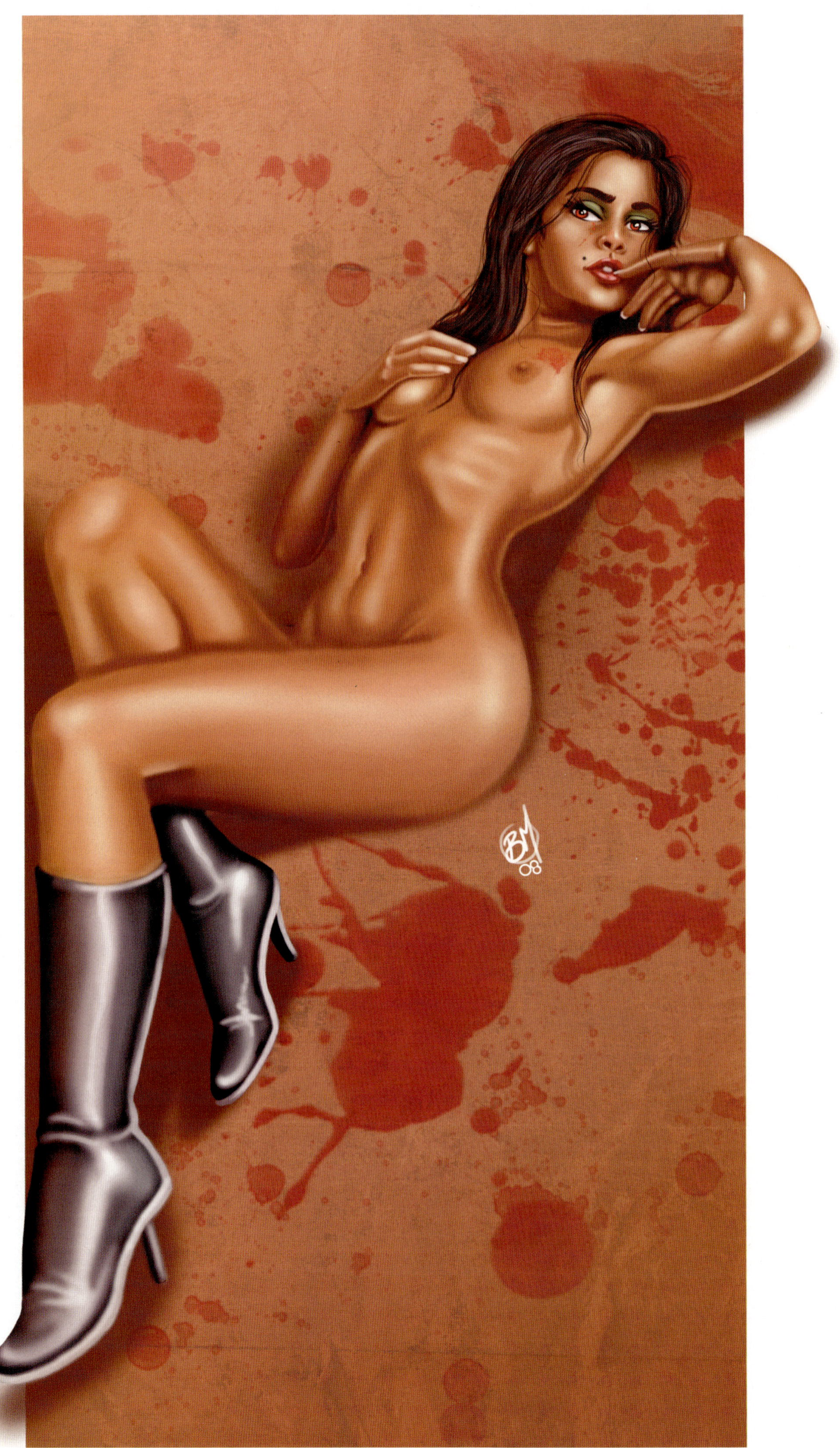

Dinner is Served

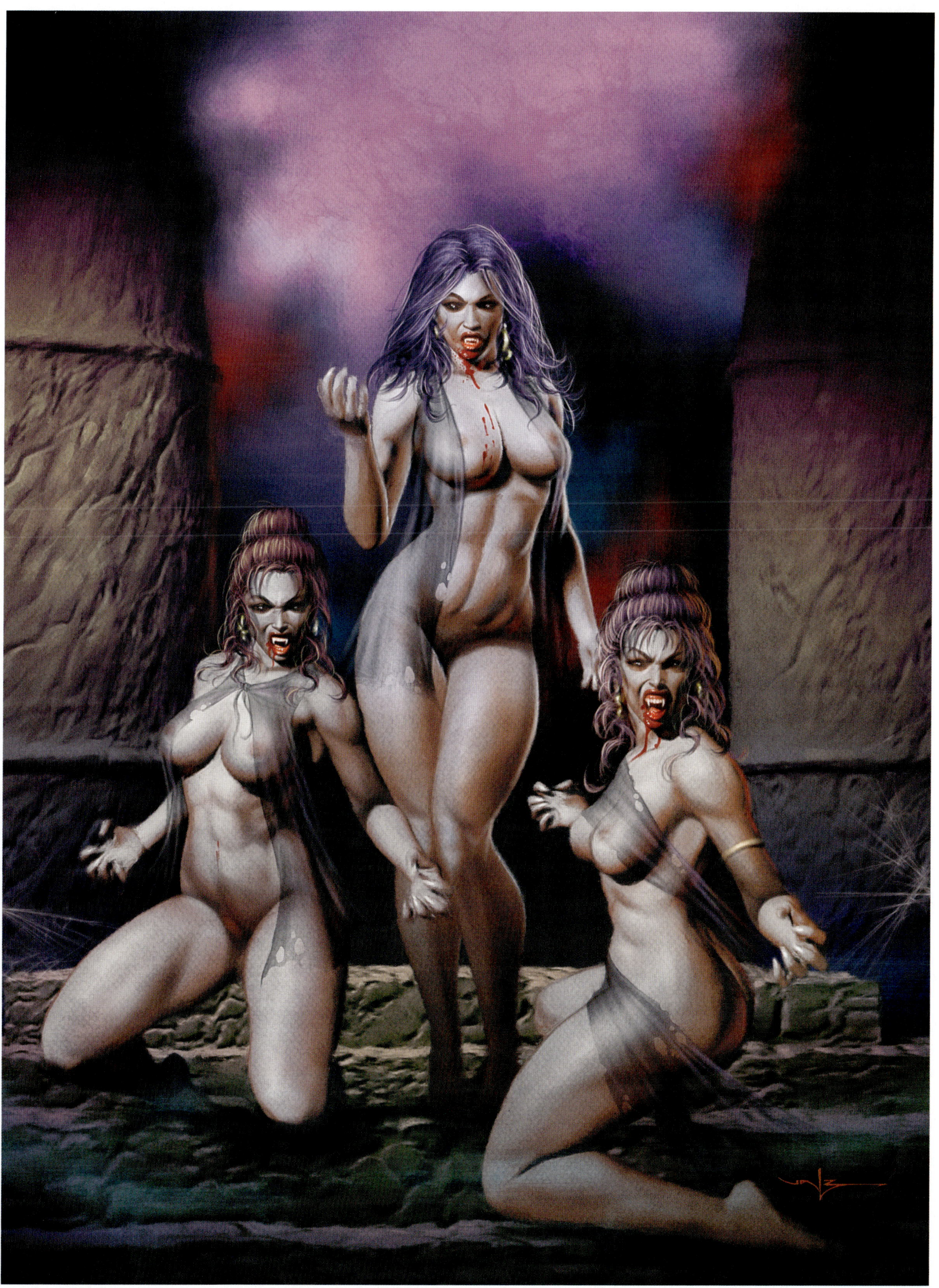

Girls Night Out

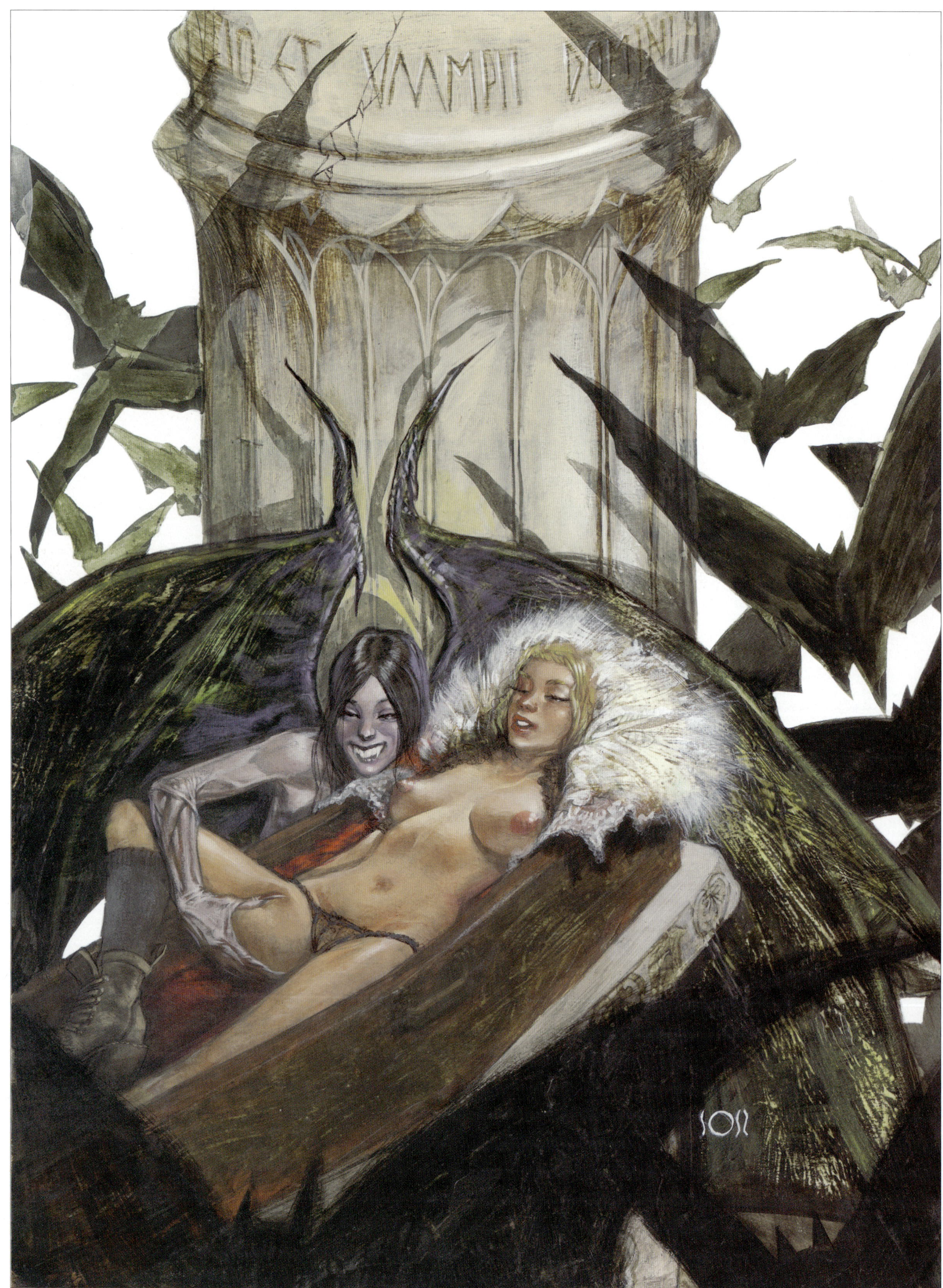

Arise

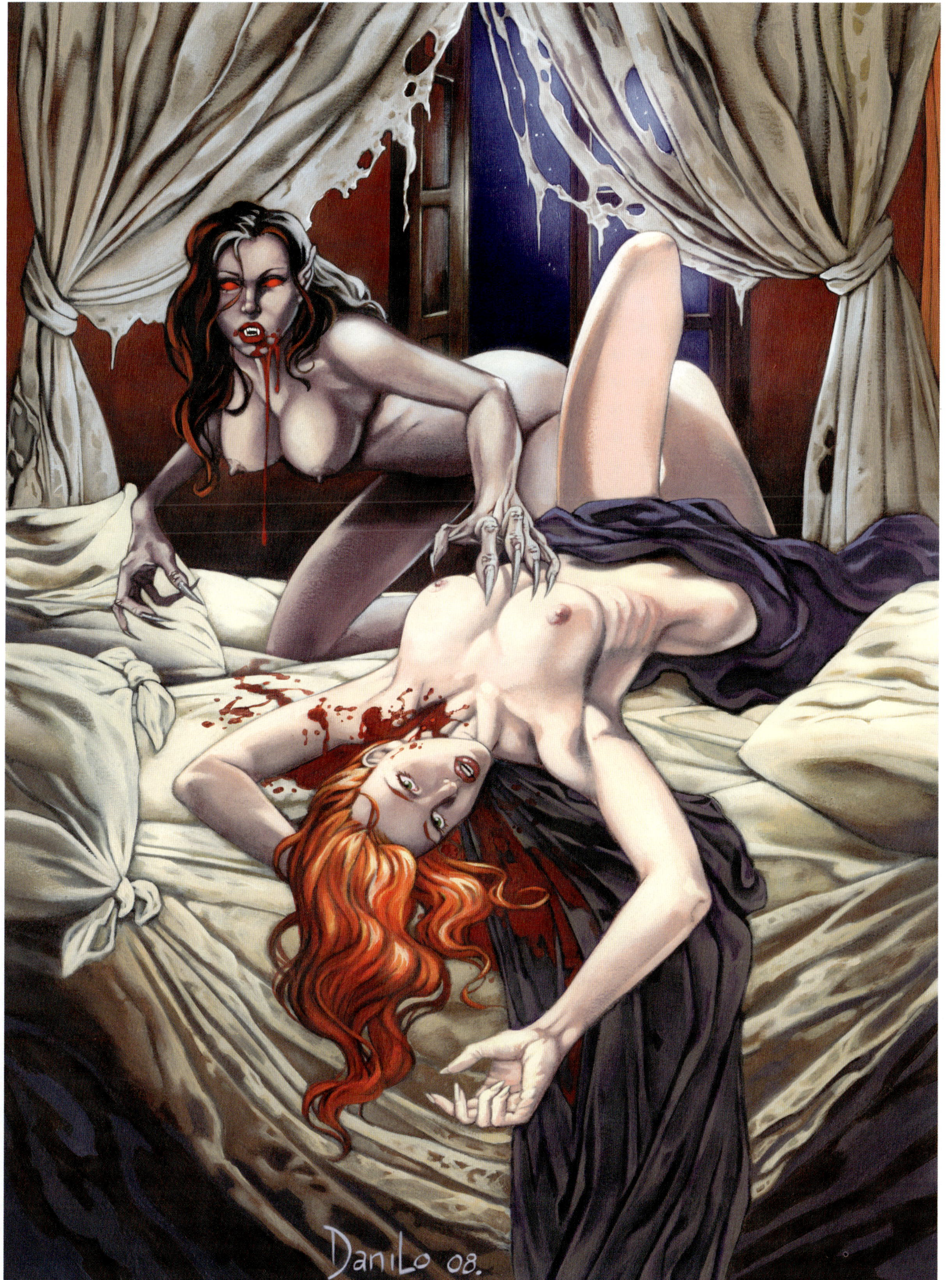

The Feeding

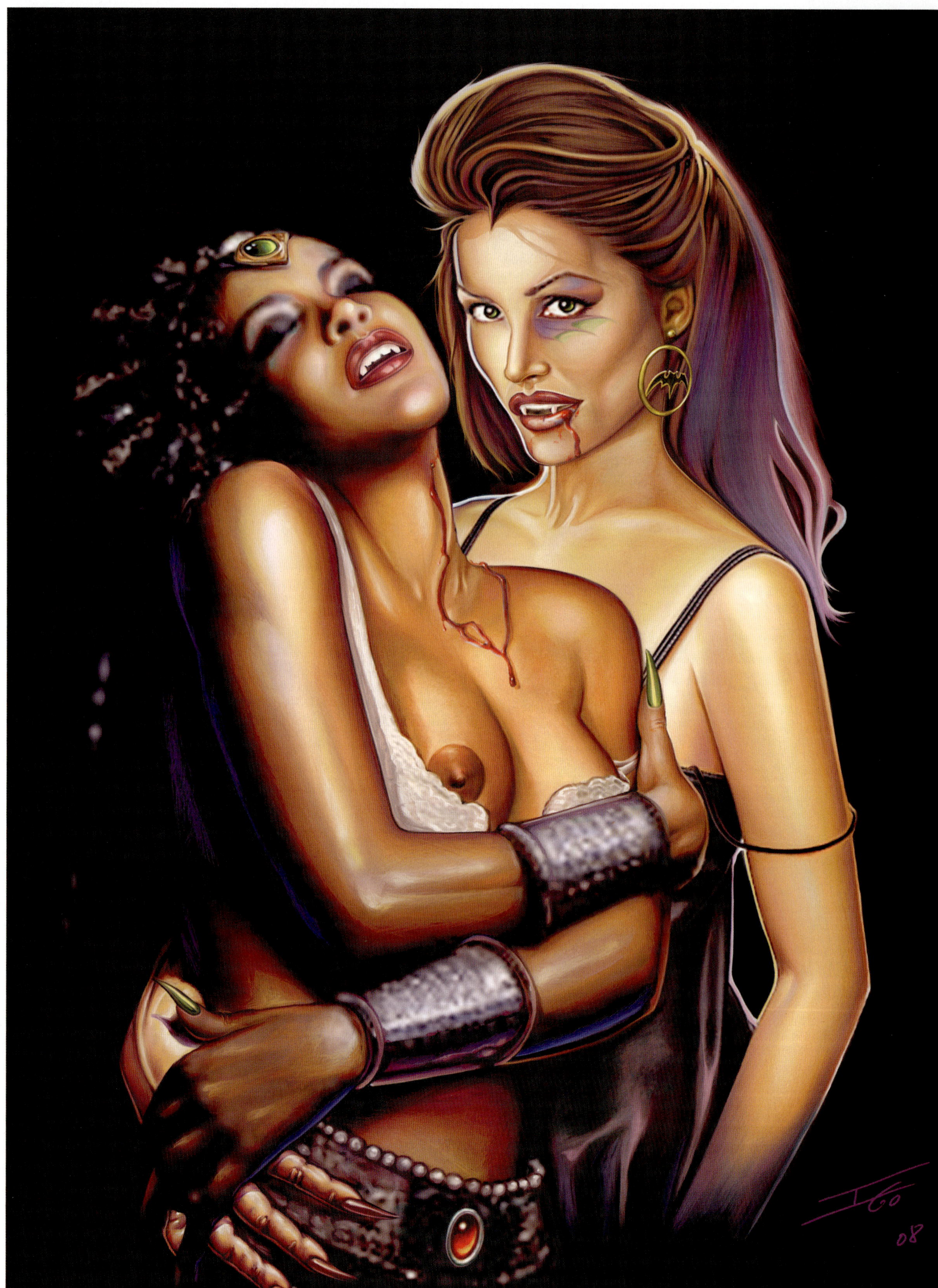

Red Rapture

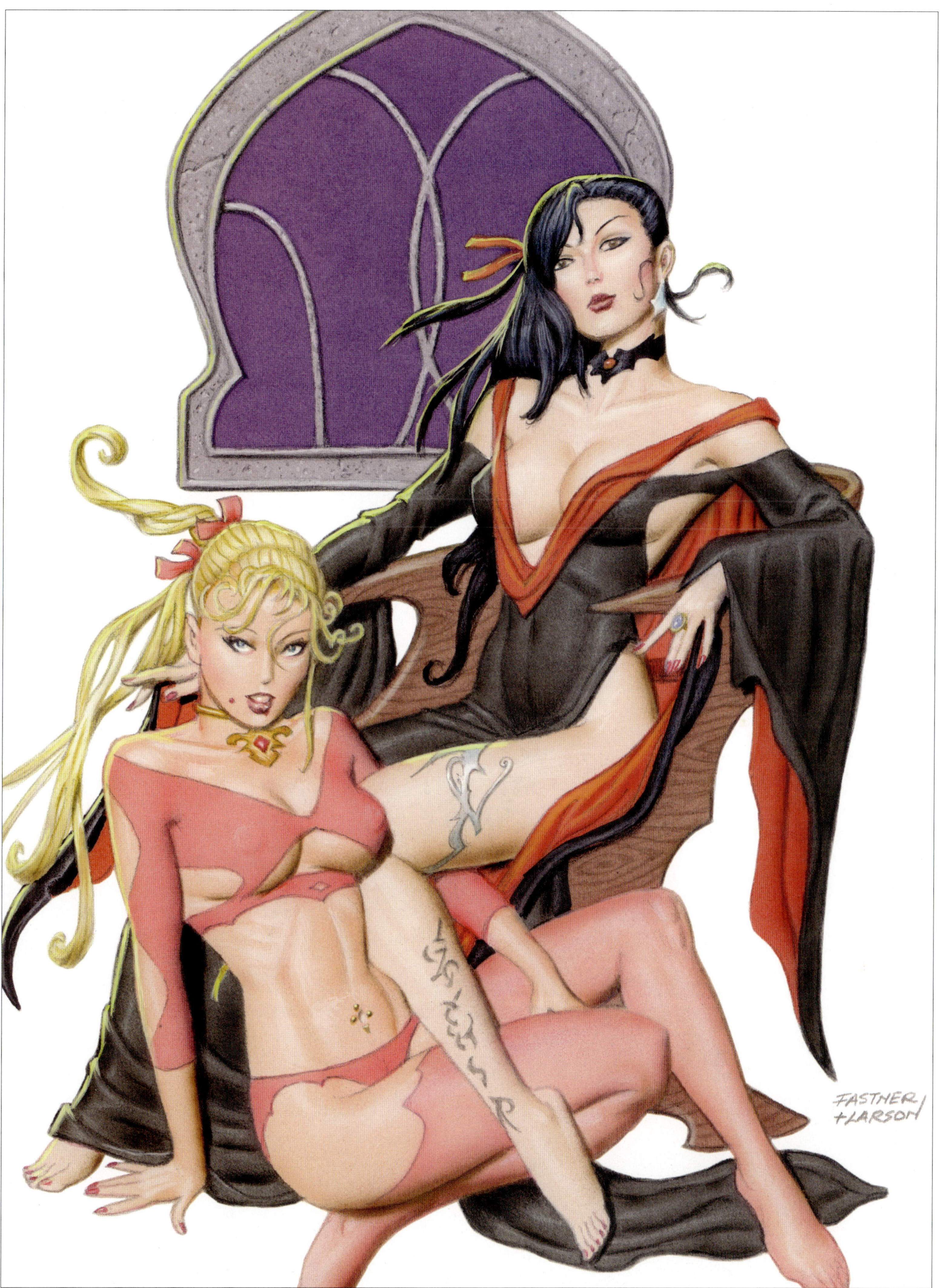

Apt Pupil

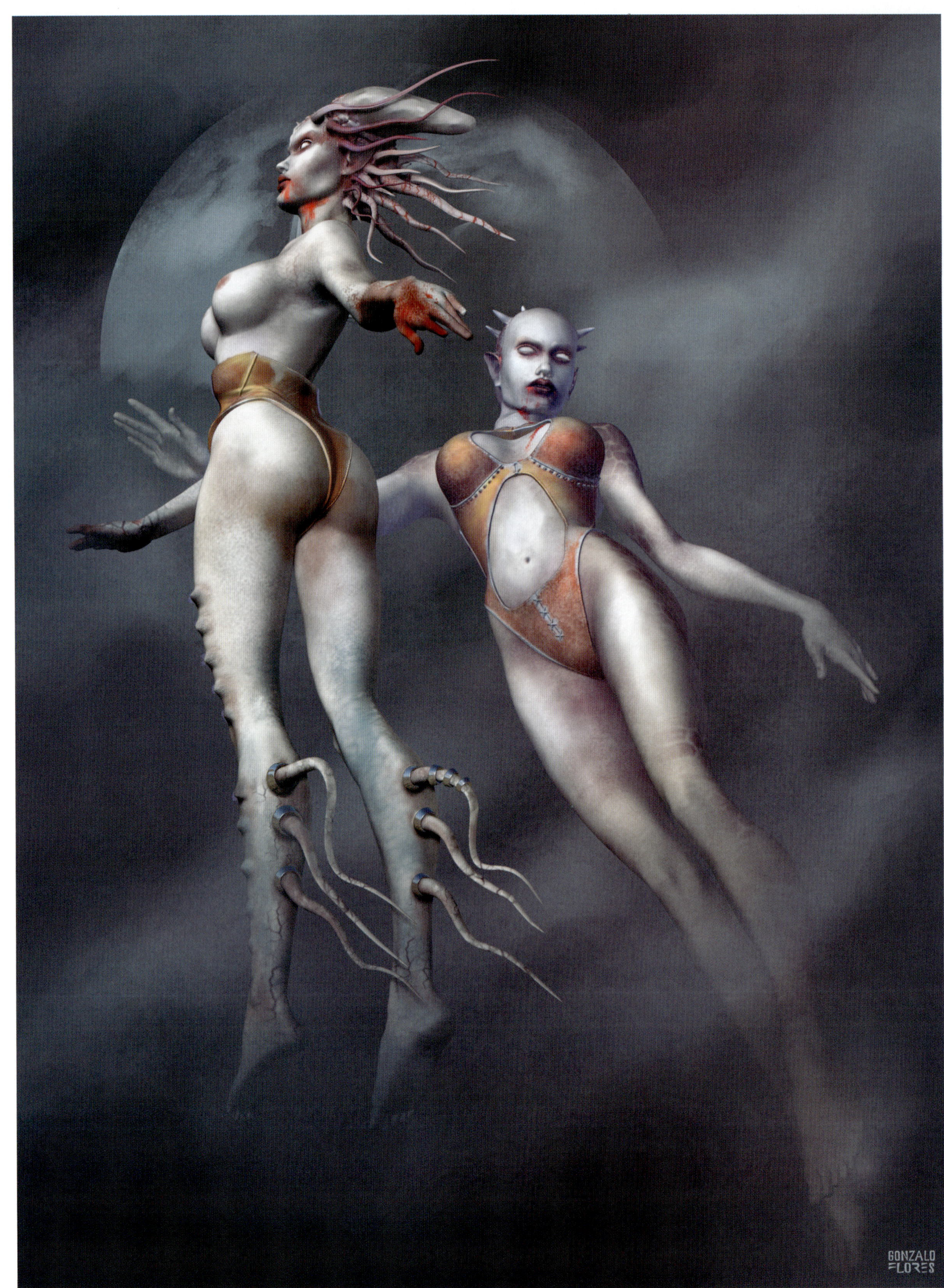

Undead and Uncaring

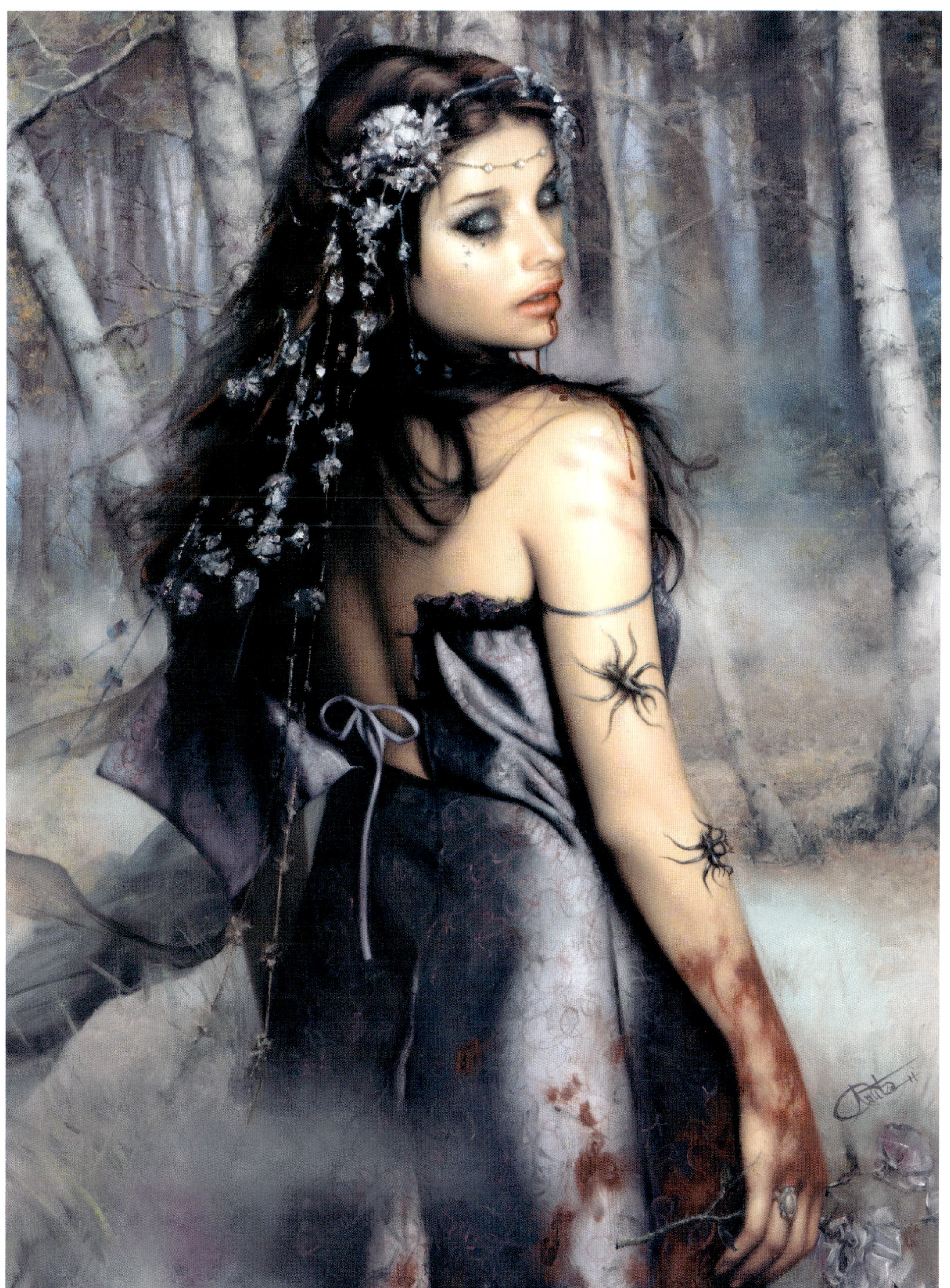

Little Pets

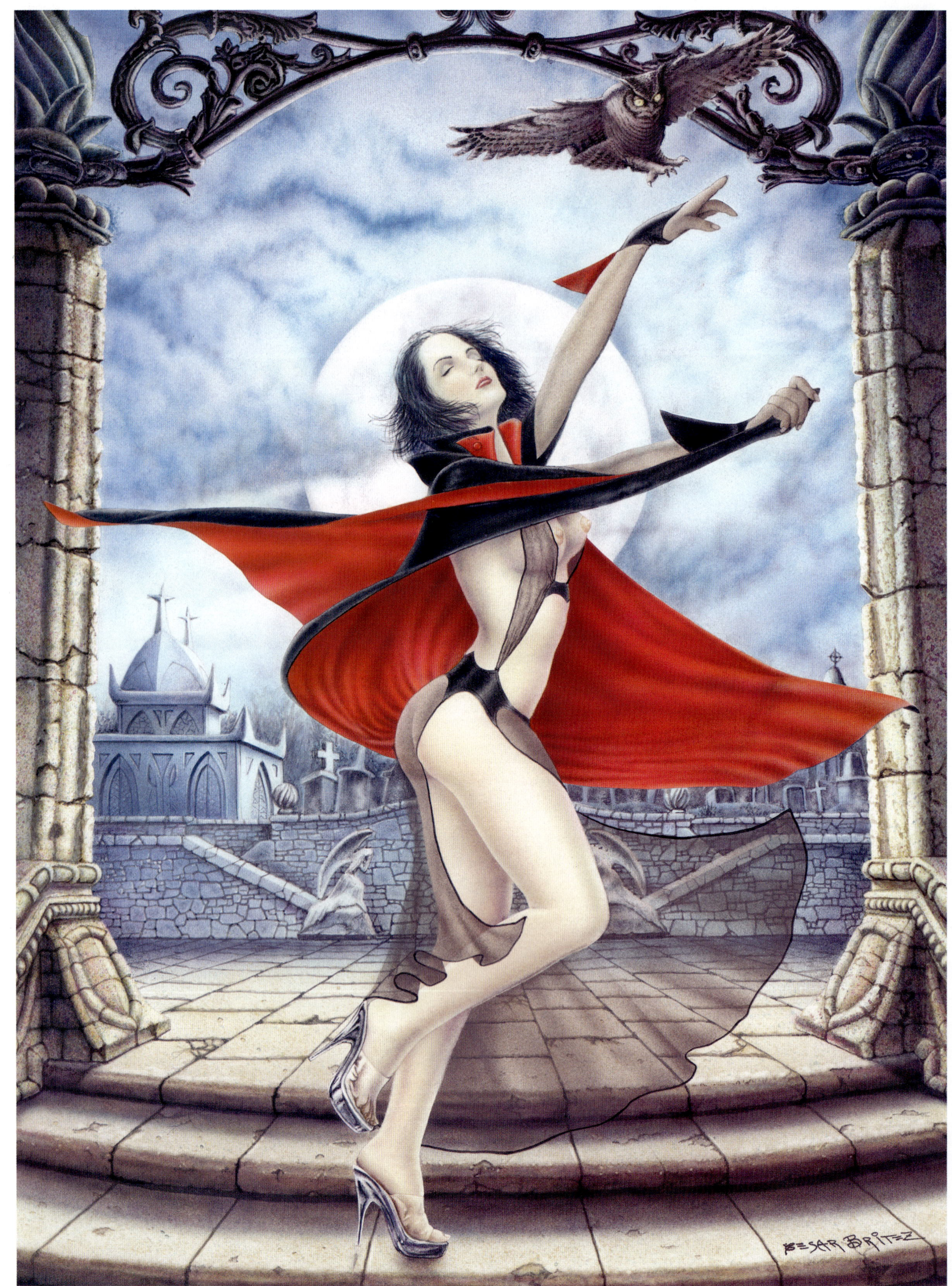

Full Moon Rising

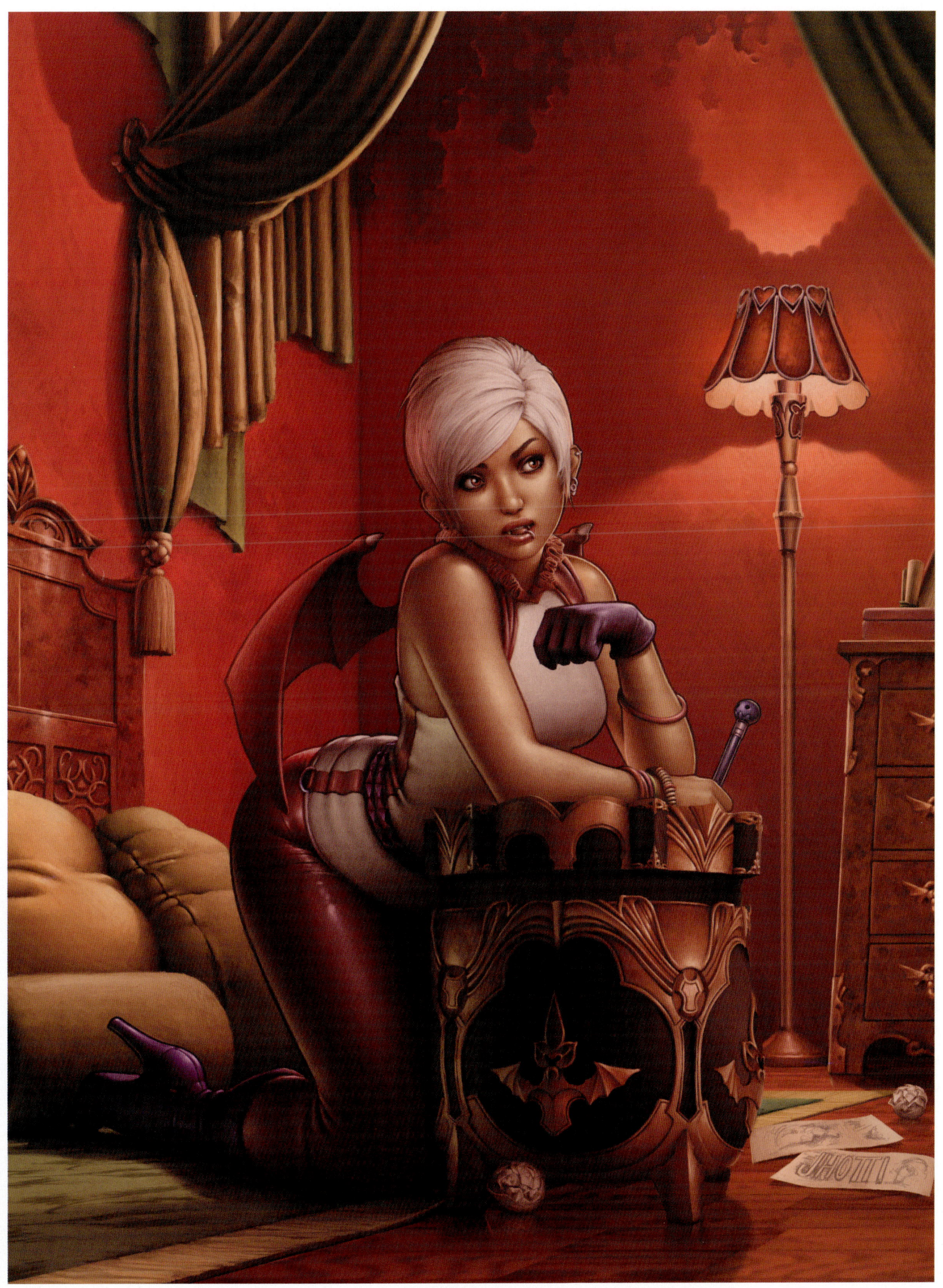

"Dear Dracula..."

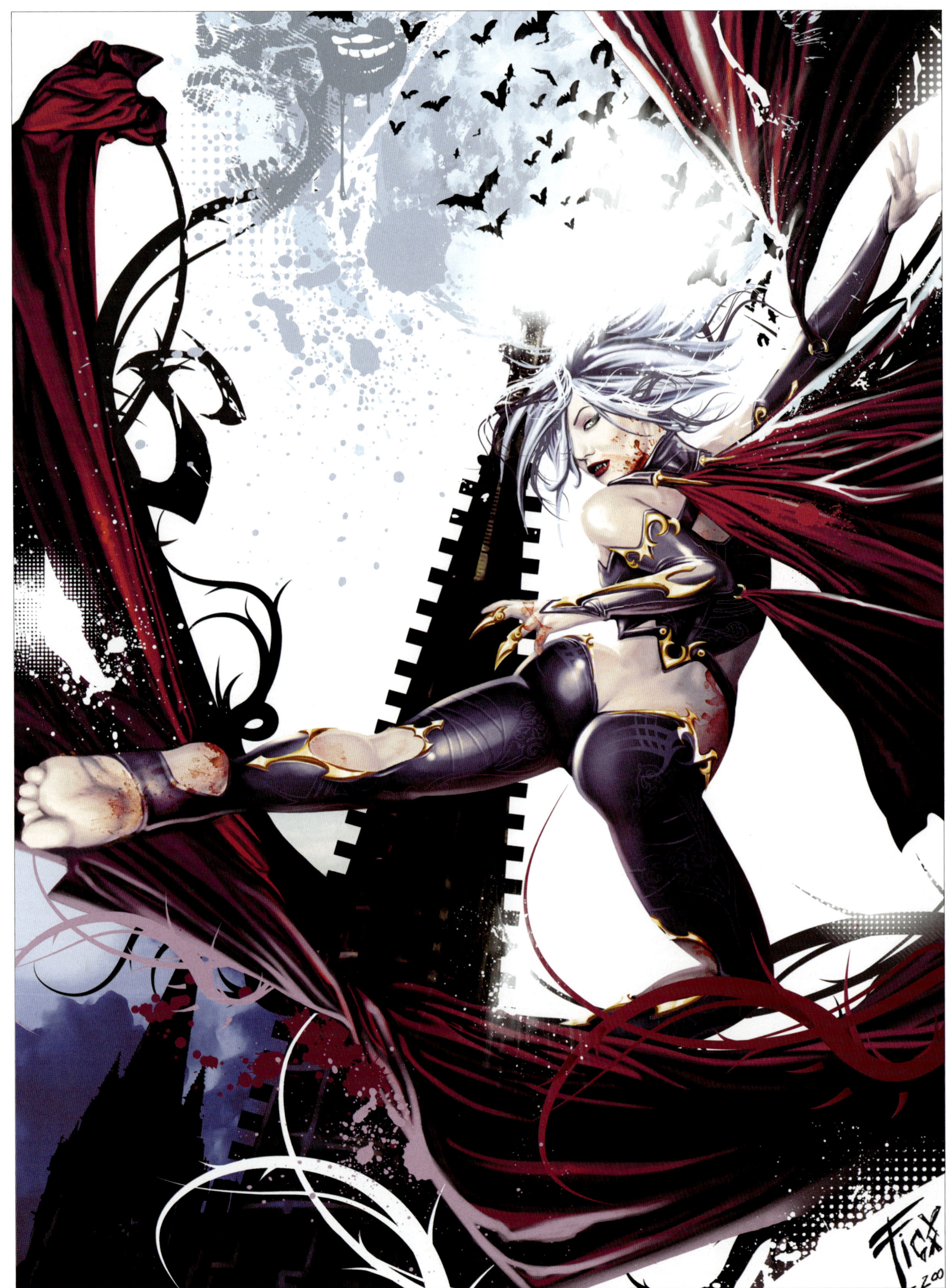

Shred the Night

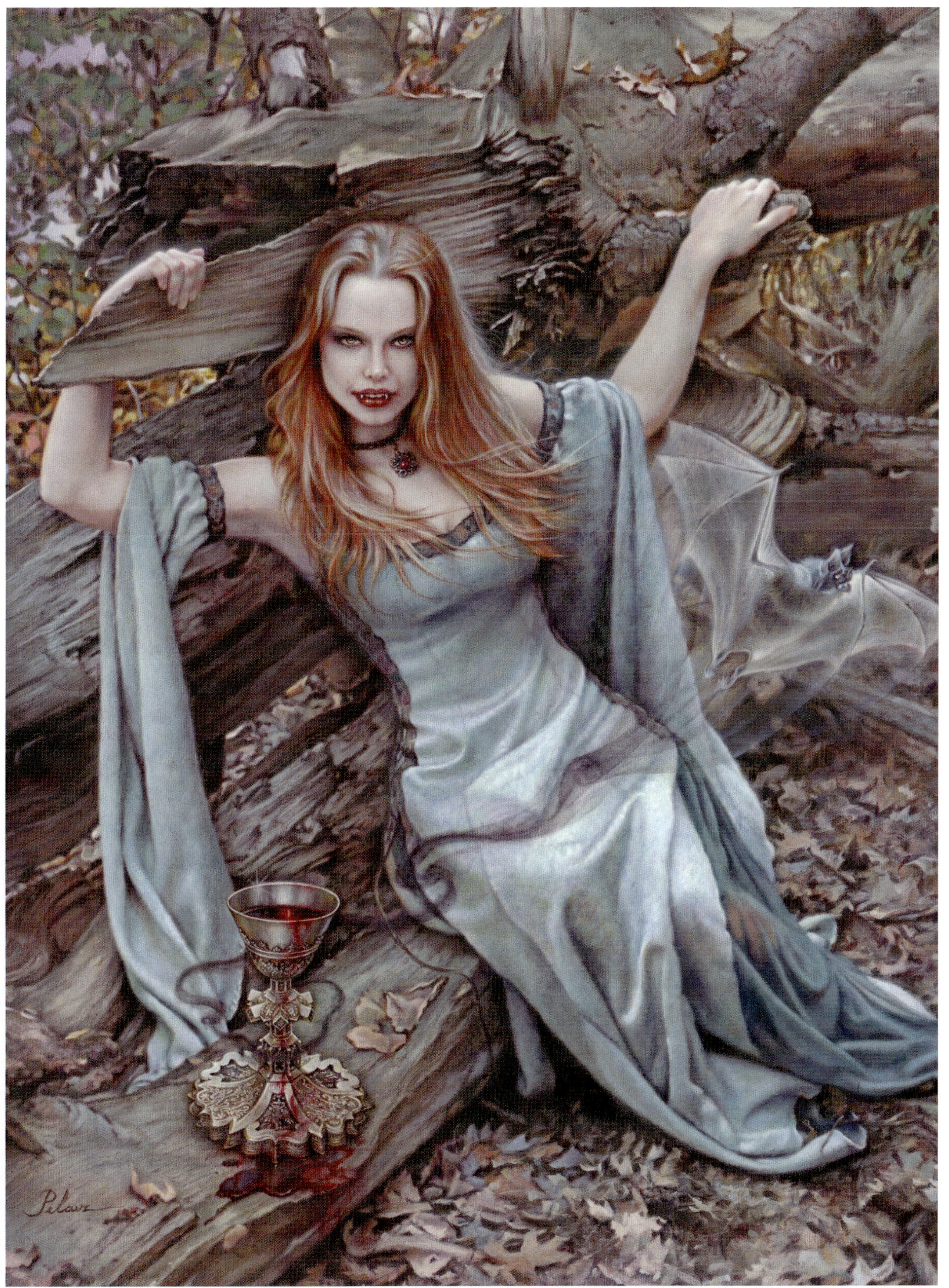

Her Secret Garden

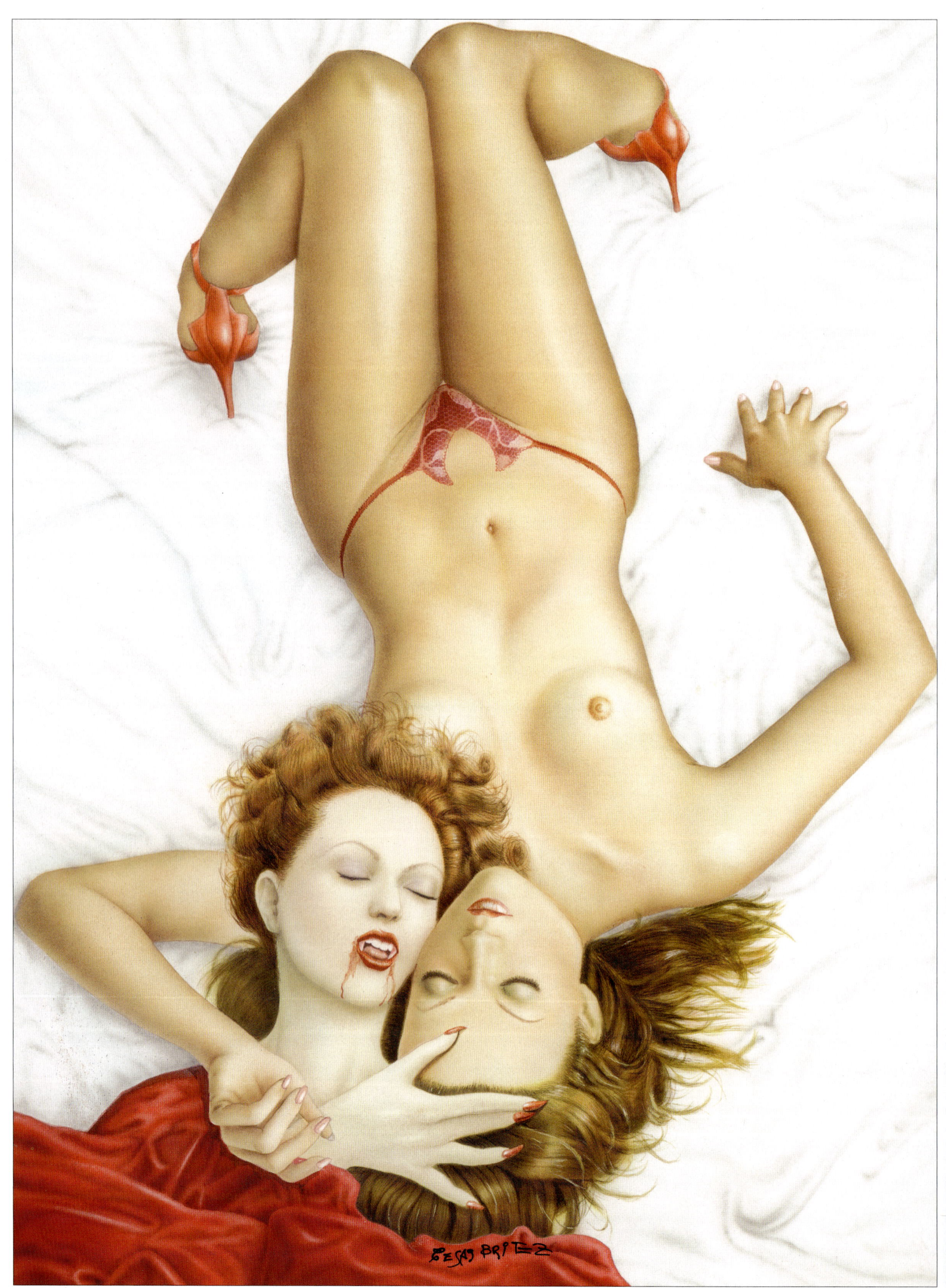

An Eternal Embrace

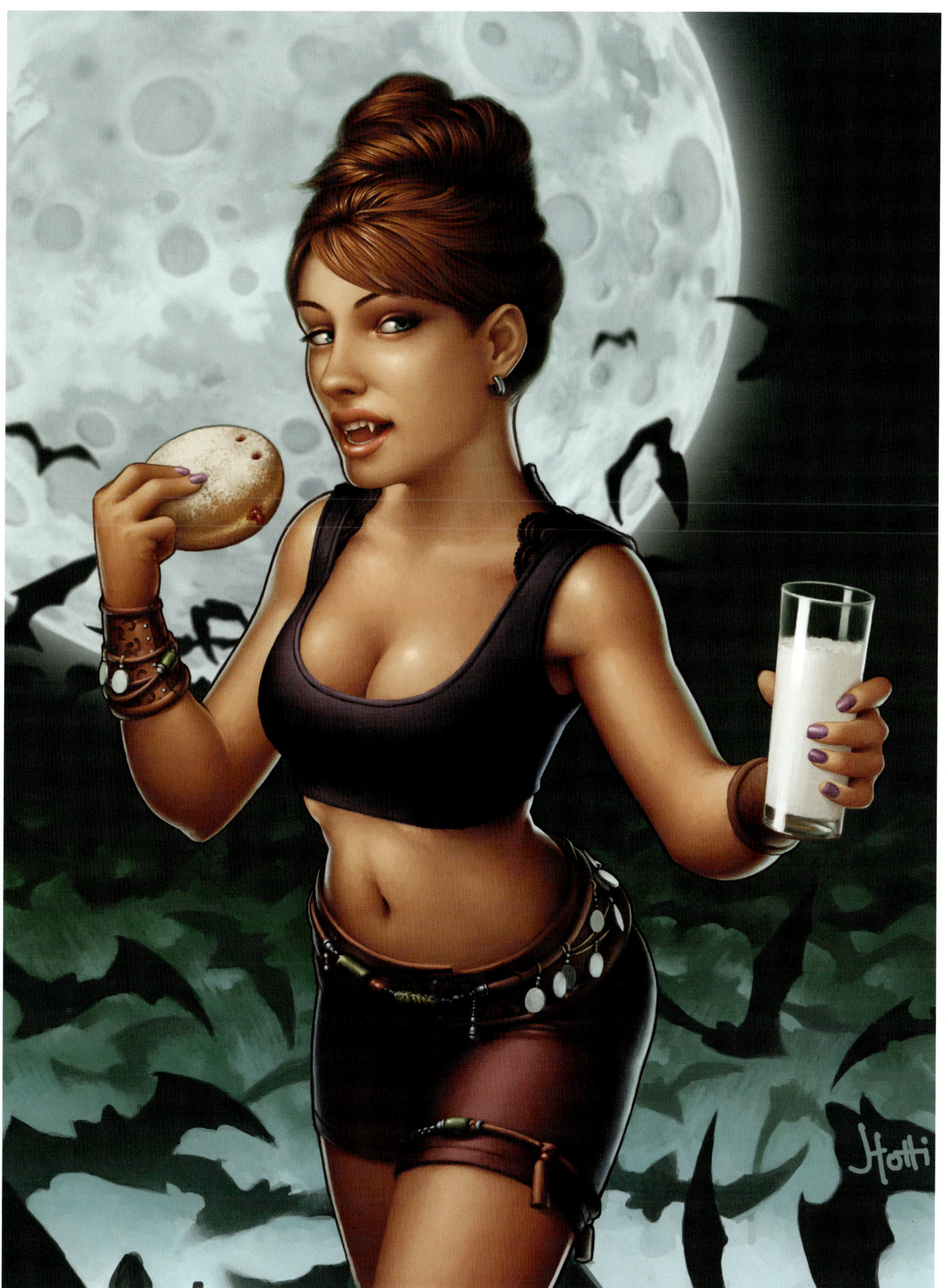

The Occasional Sweet Treat!

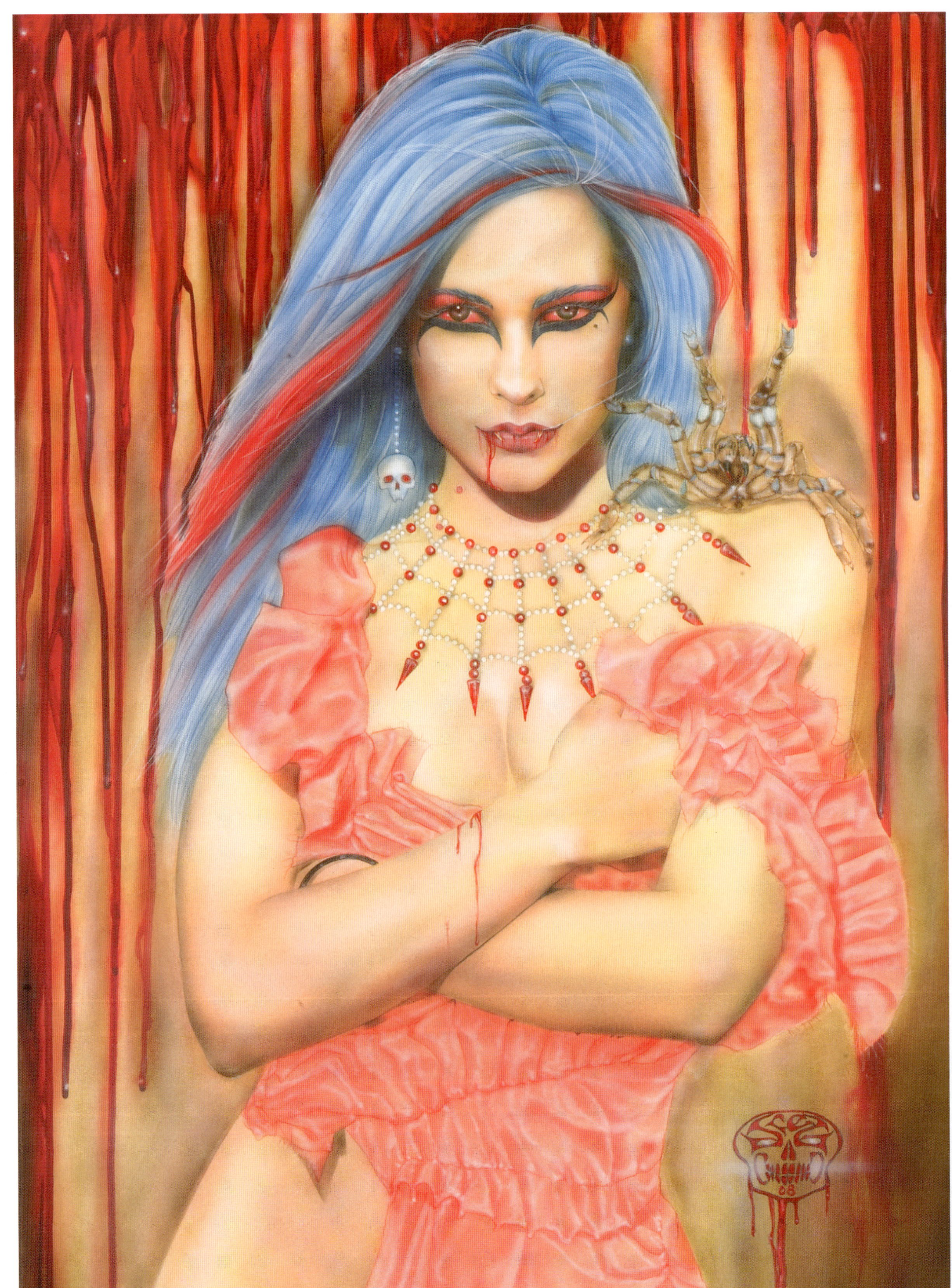

Blood Runs Cold

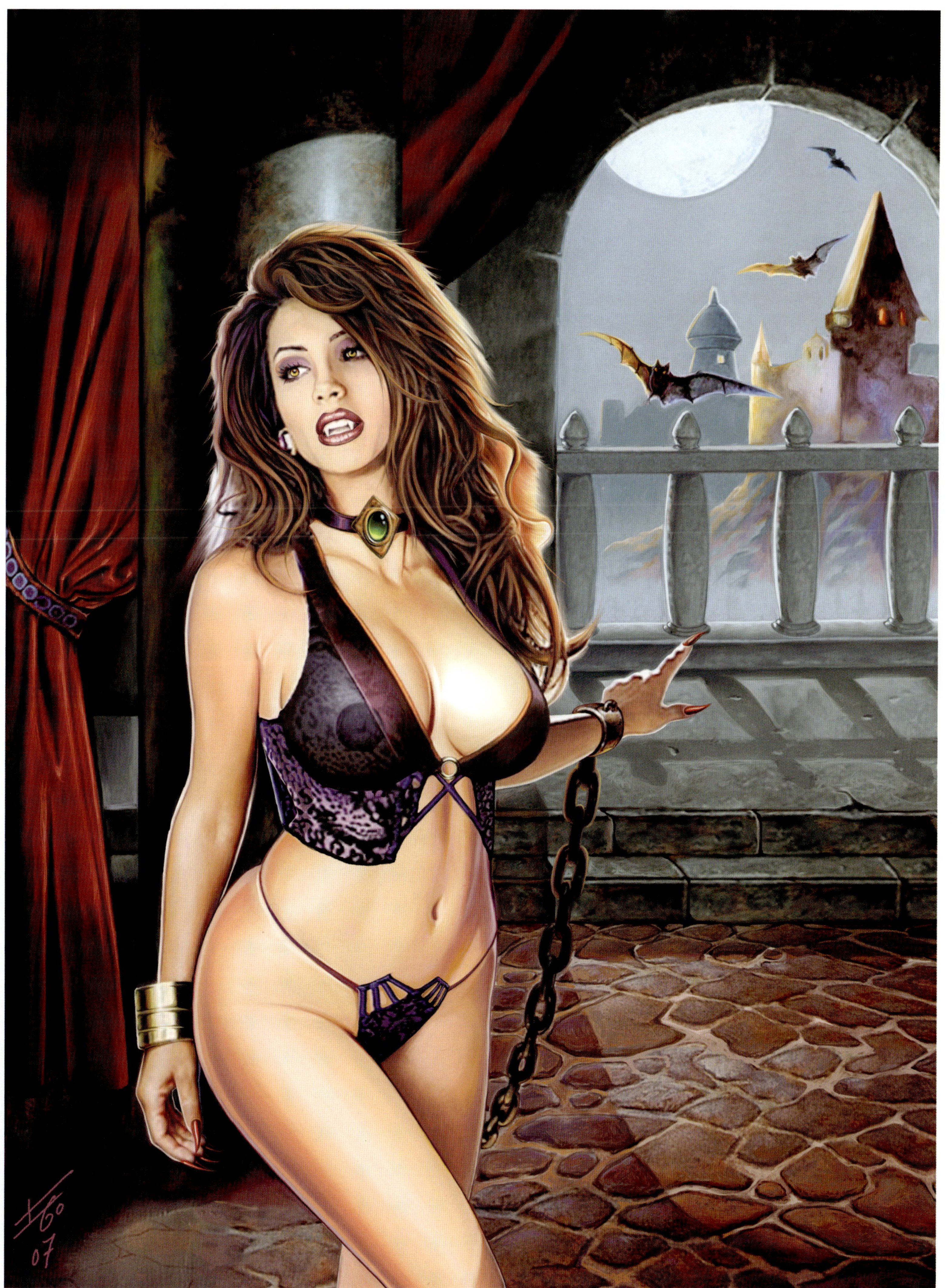

Forbidden by Her Master

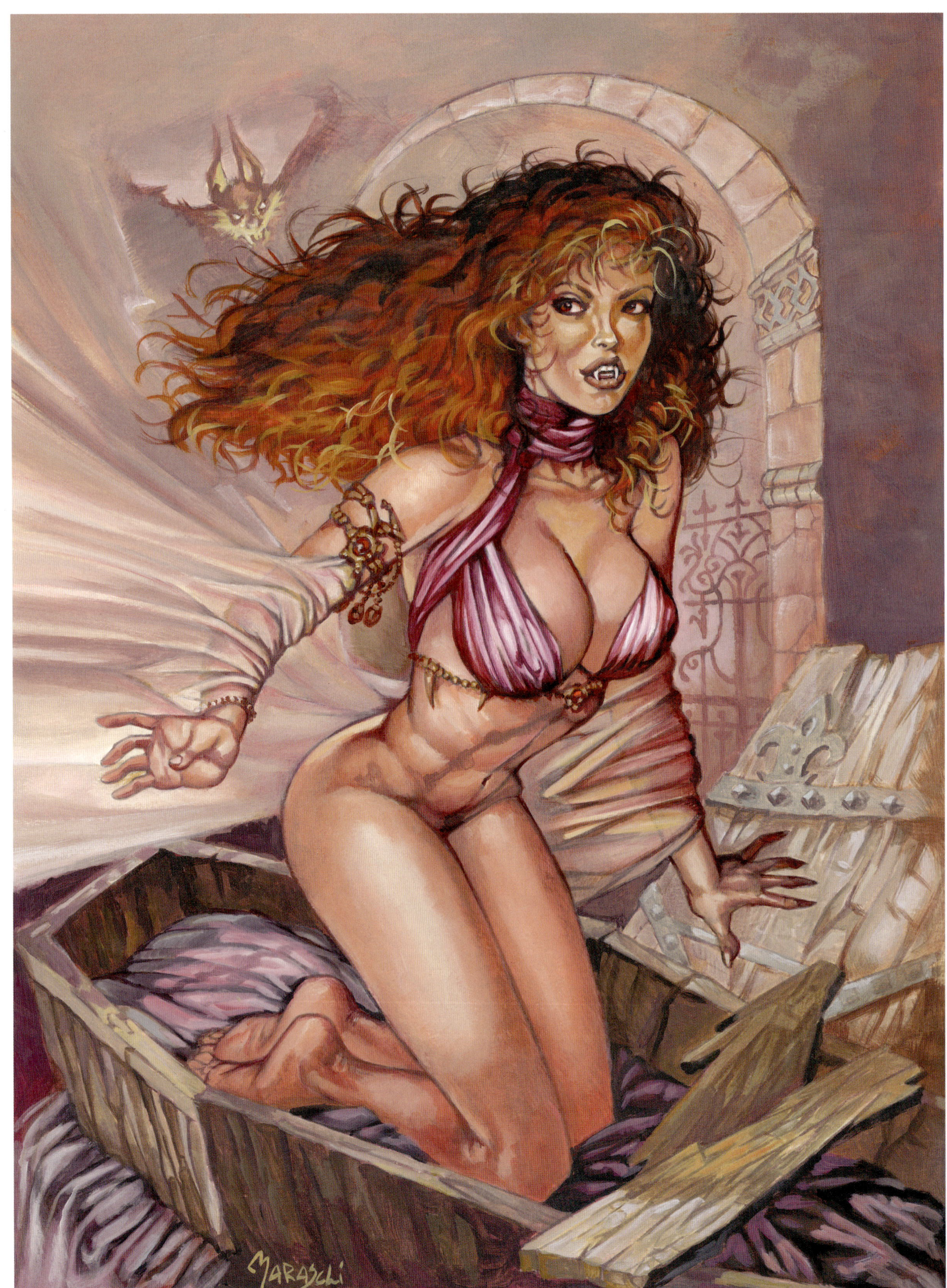

The Night Beckons

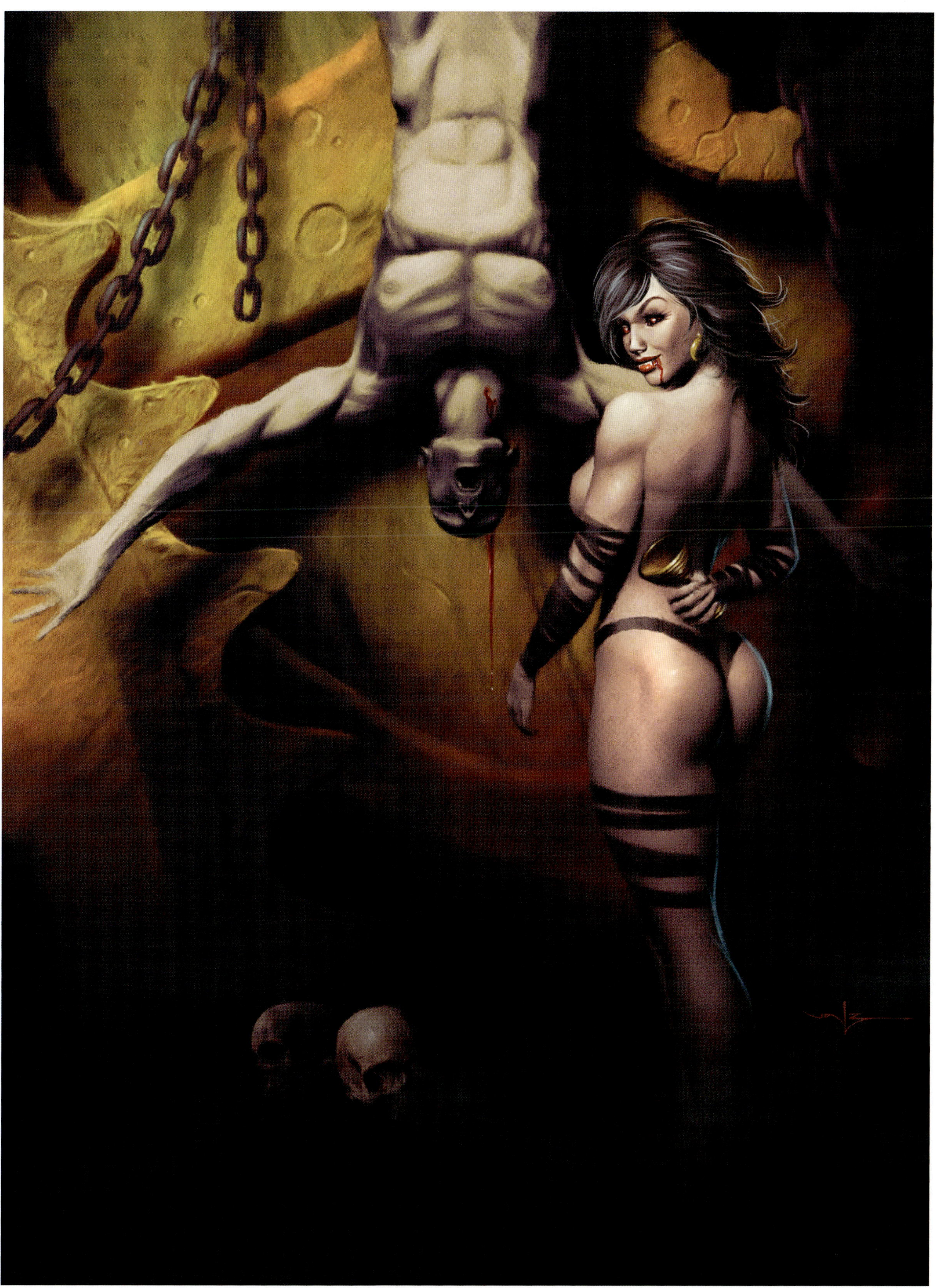

Nothing Beats Fresh-Squeezed

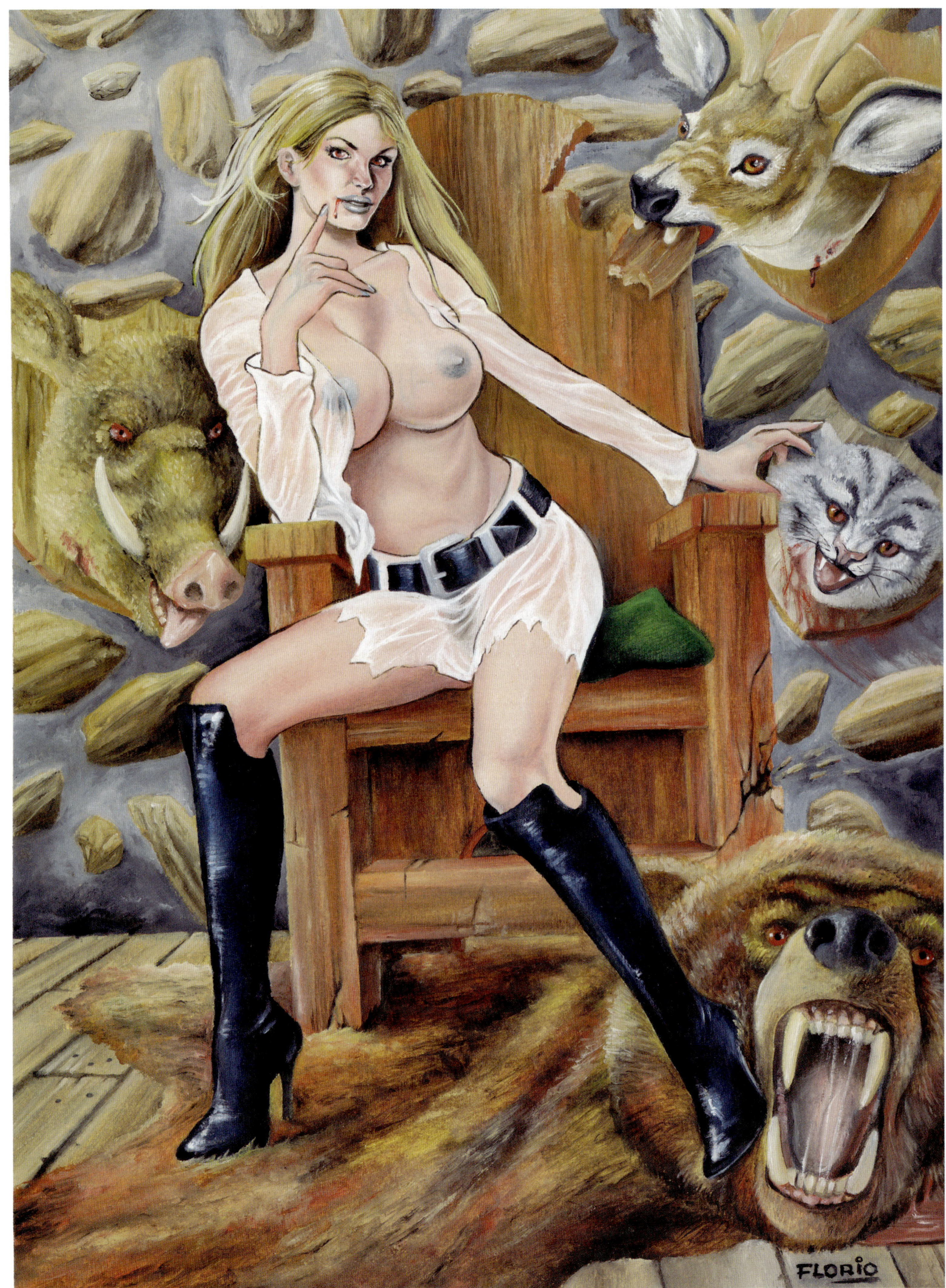

Undead Things

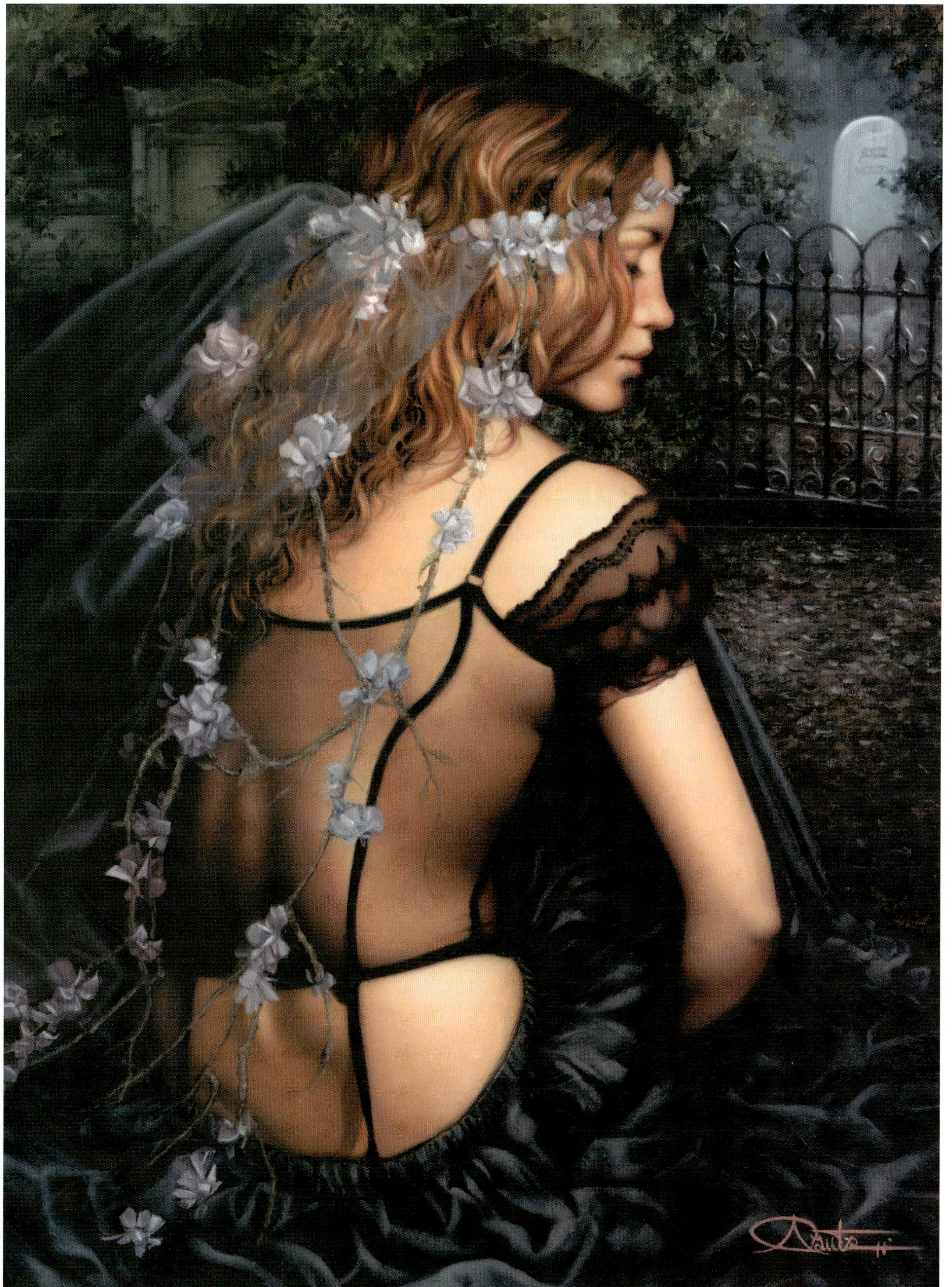

Wake the Dead

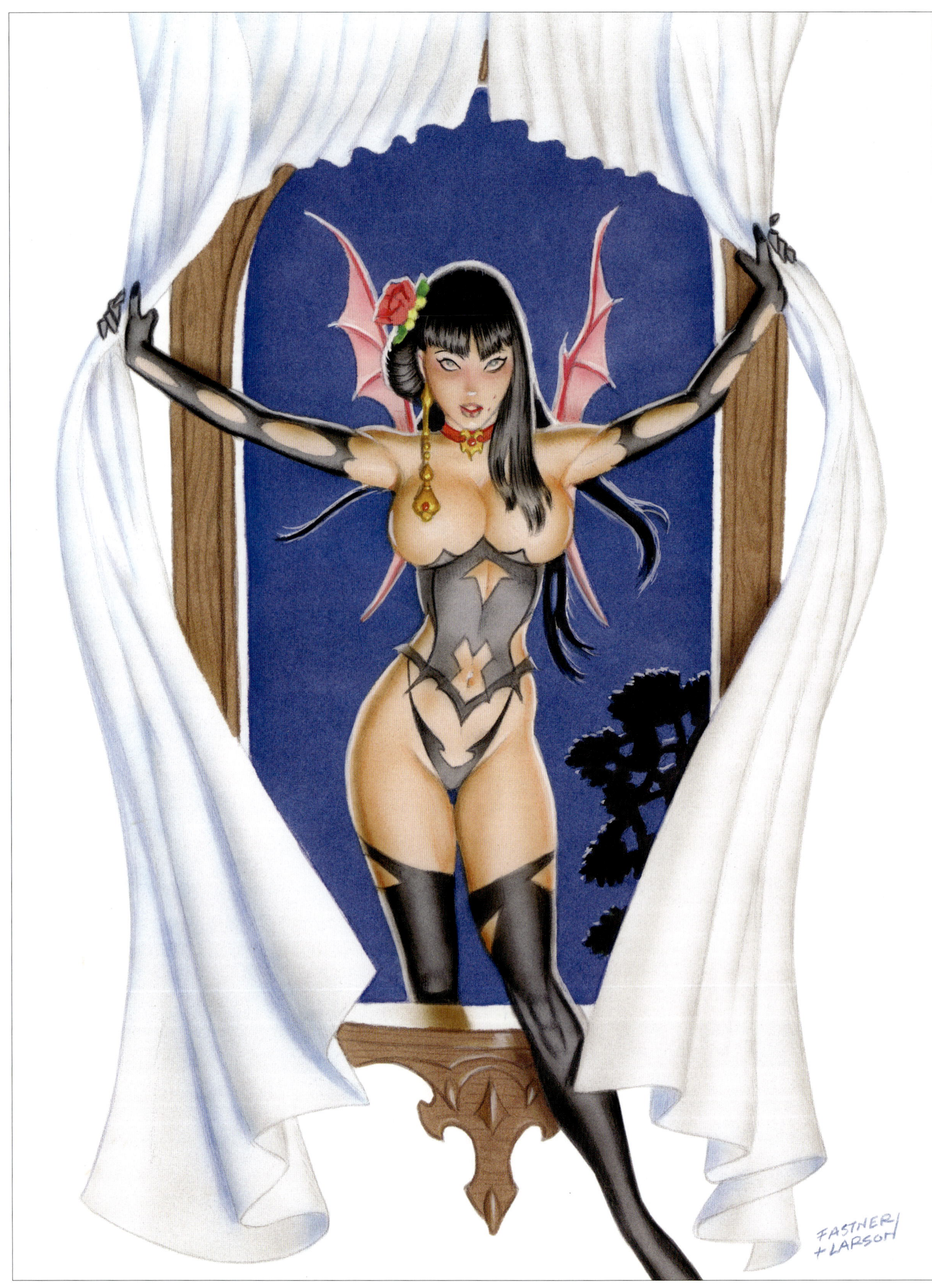

Homecoming

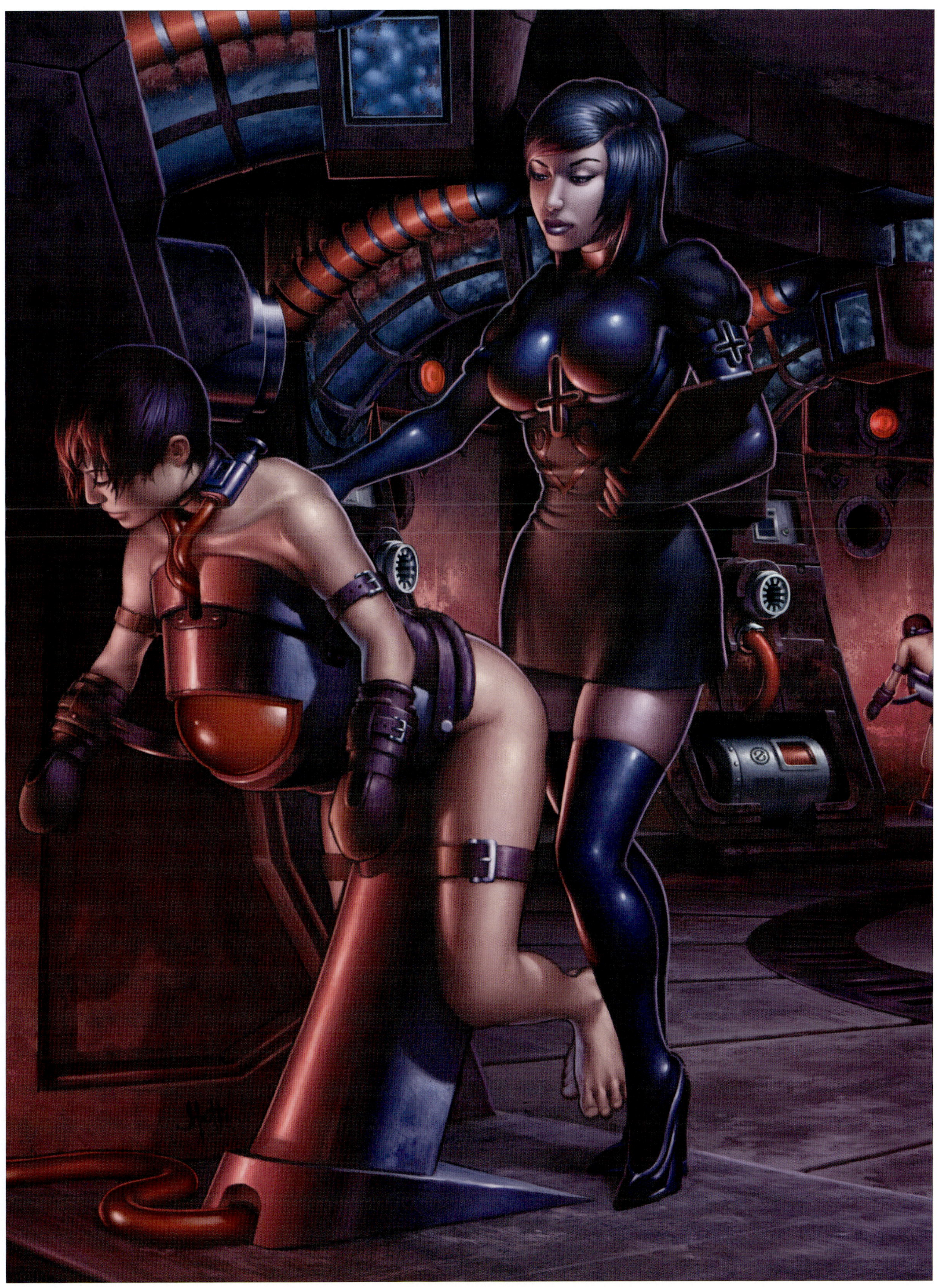

Harvest Goes Hi-Tech

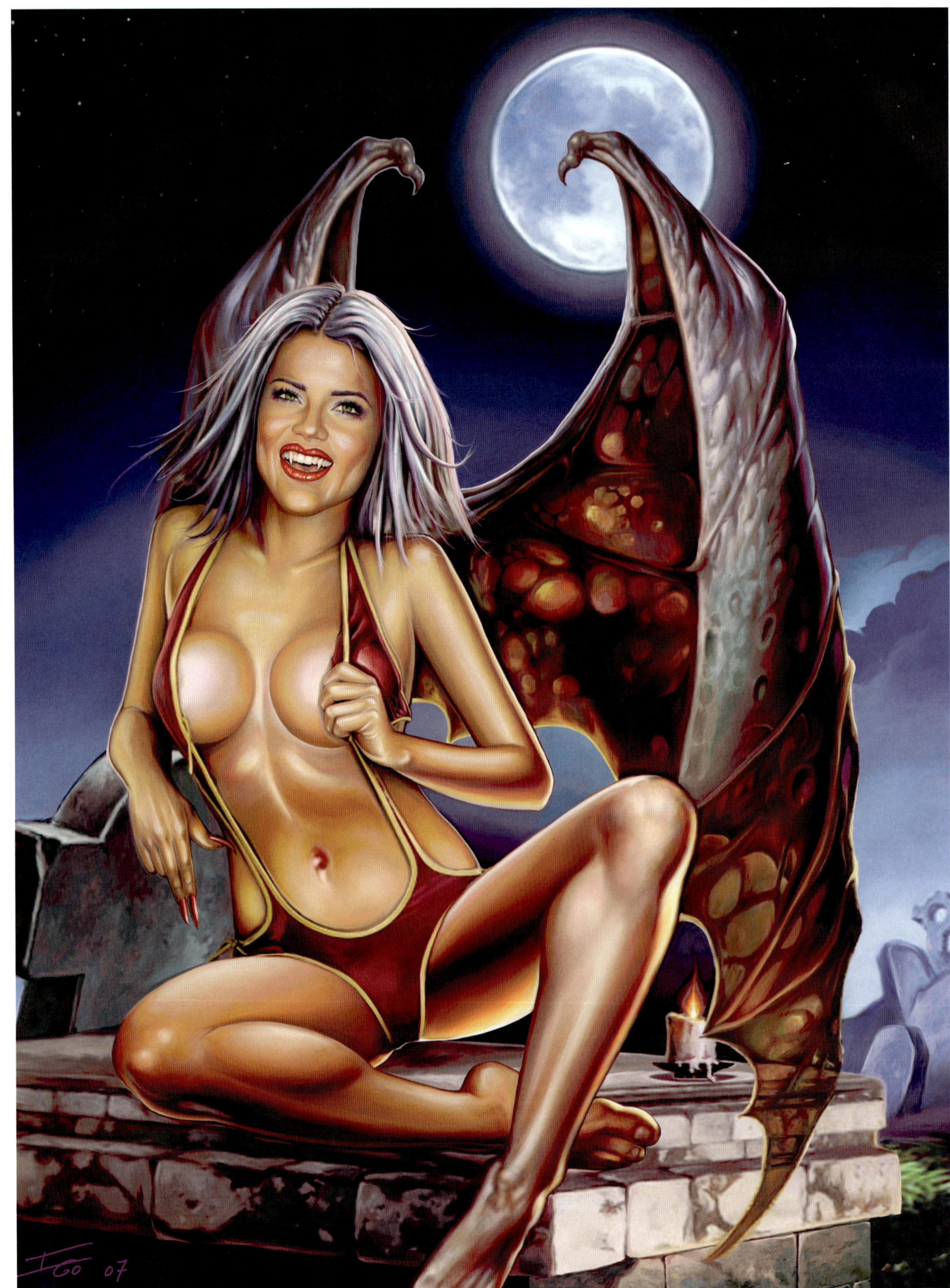

First Solo Hunt

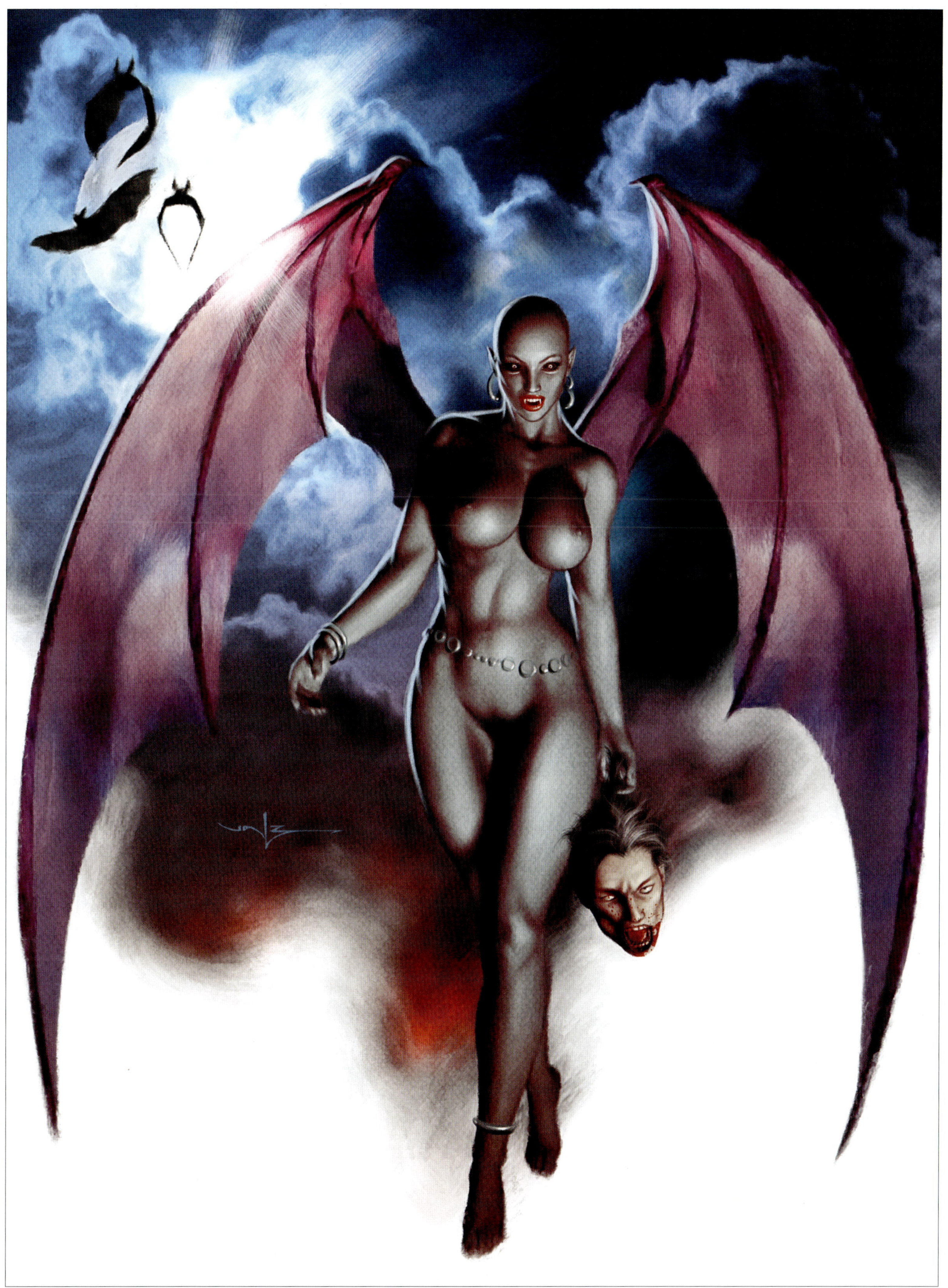

A Late Night Souvenir

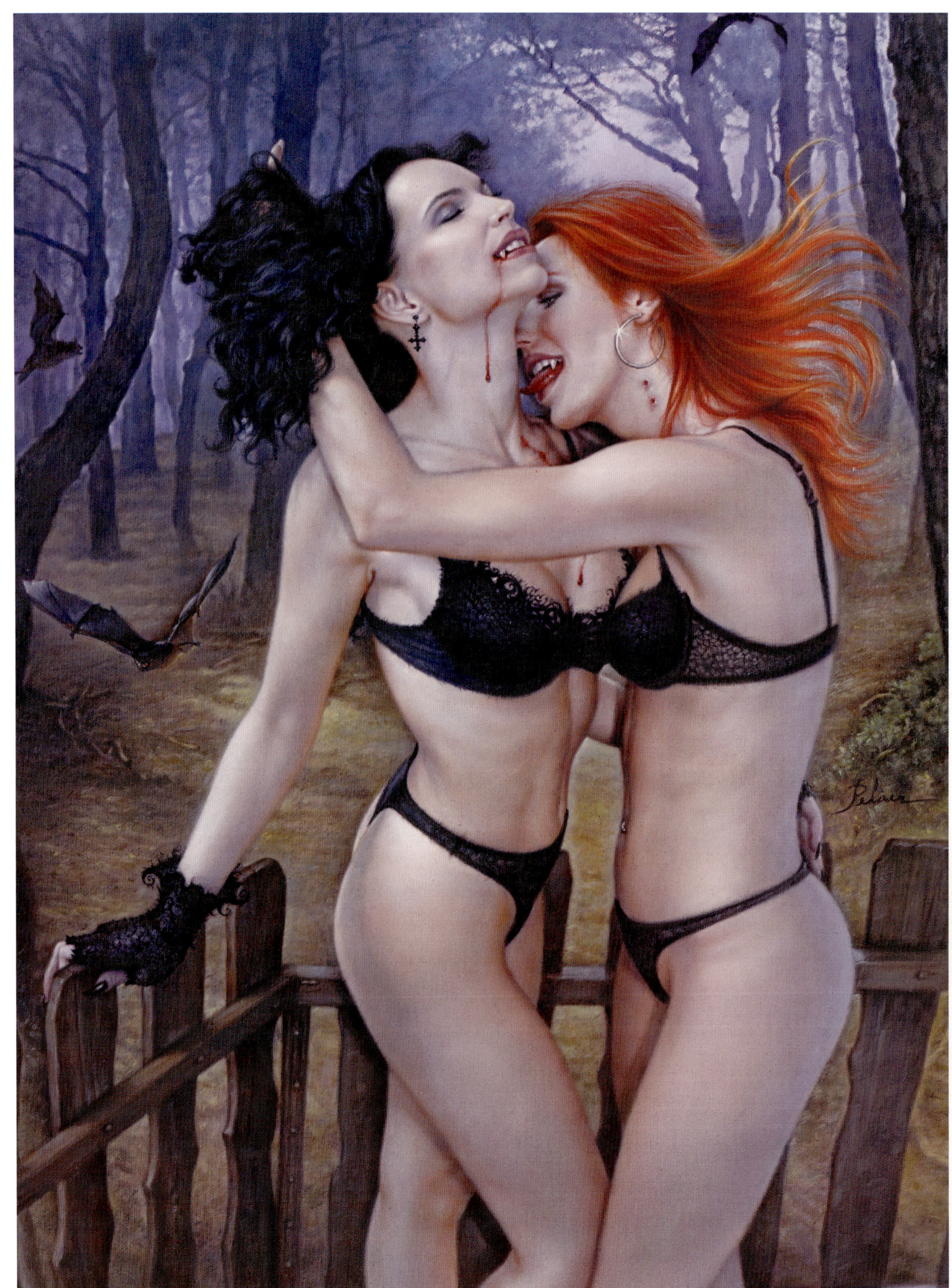

Party For Two

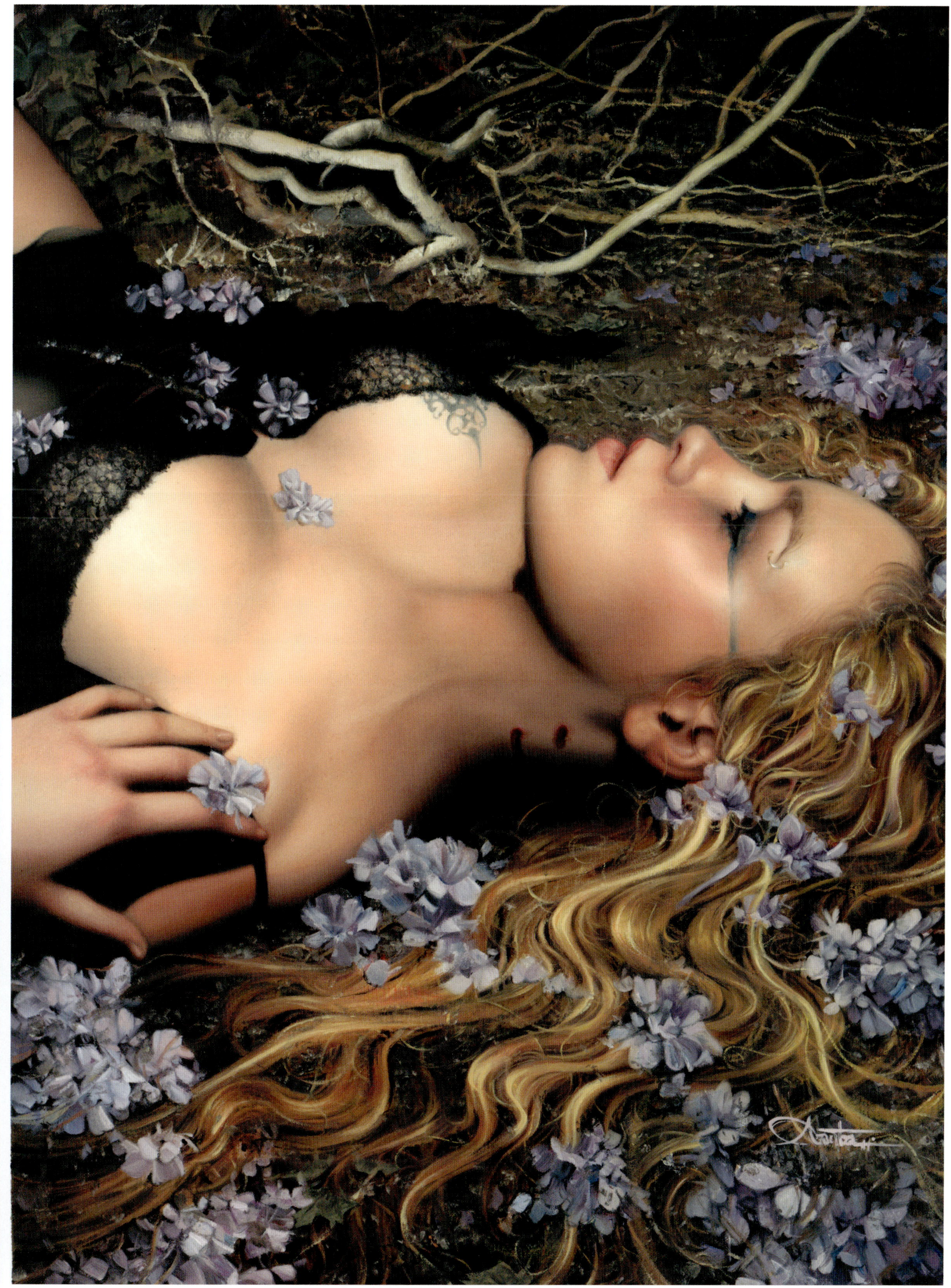

A Love That Will Never Die

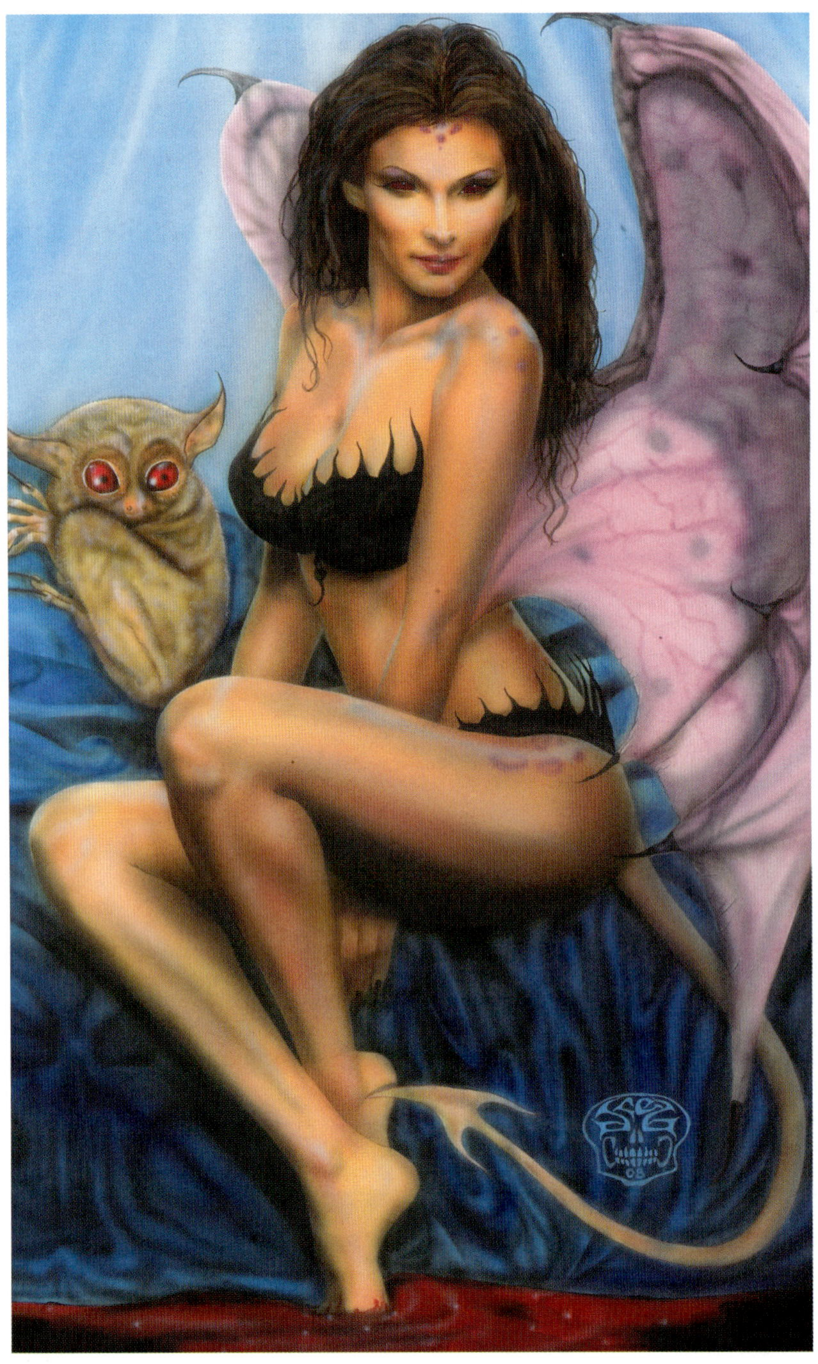

Creatures

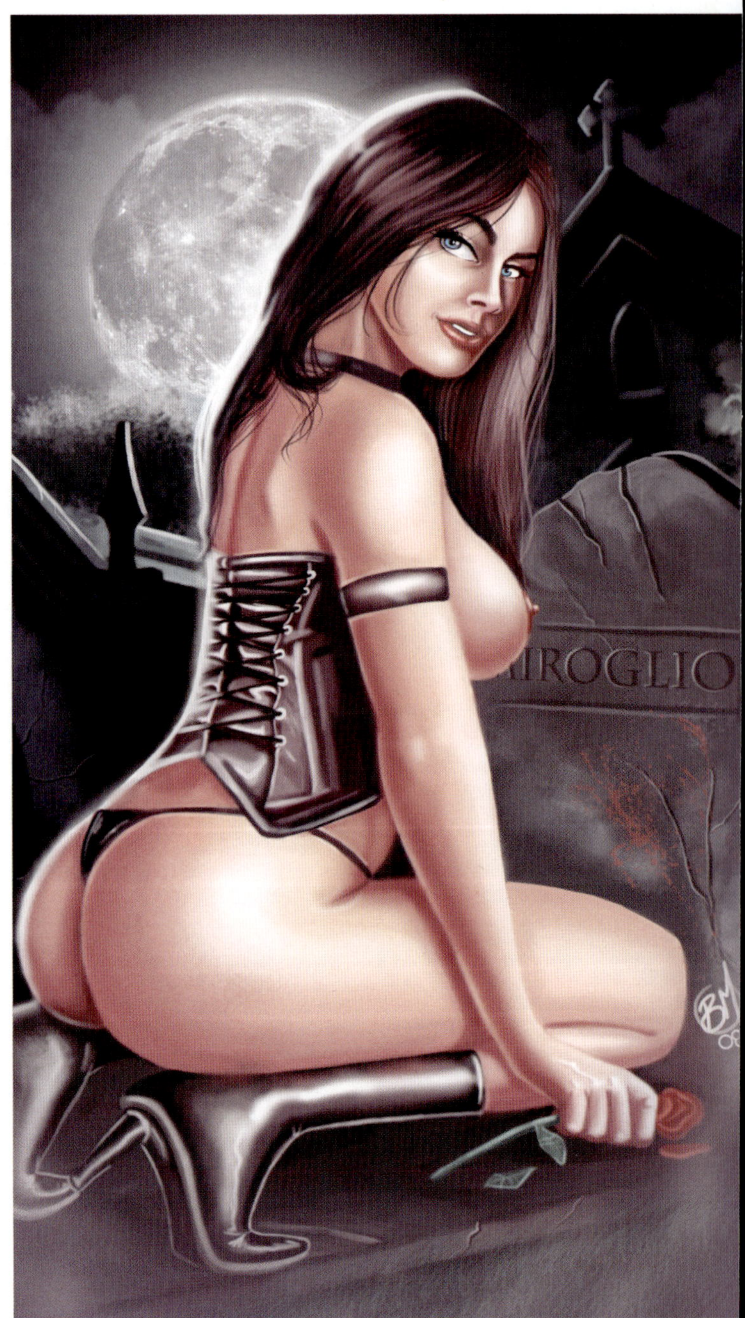

Due Respects

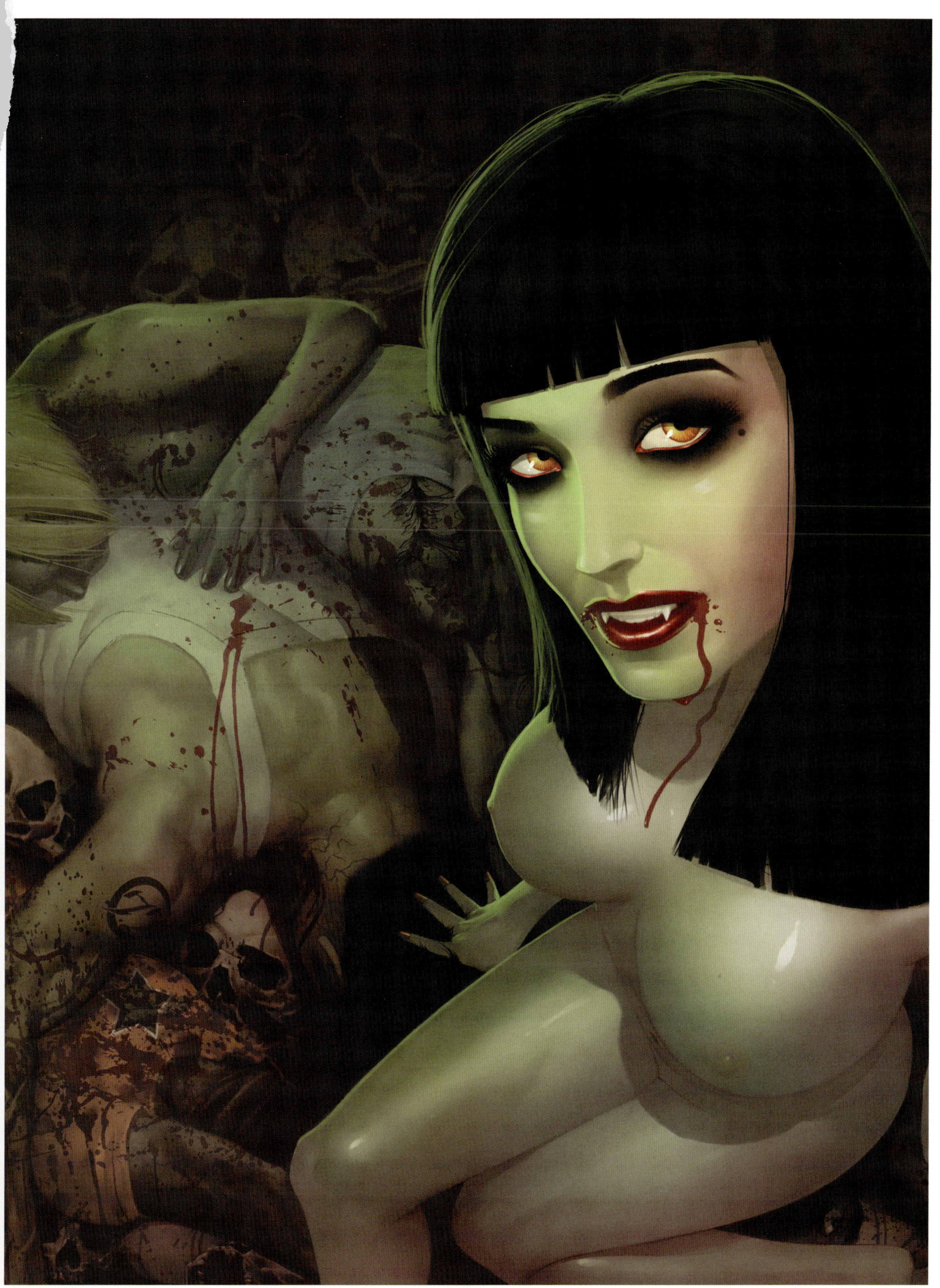

Insatiable

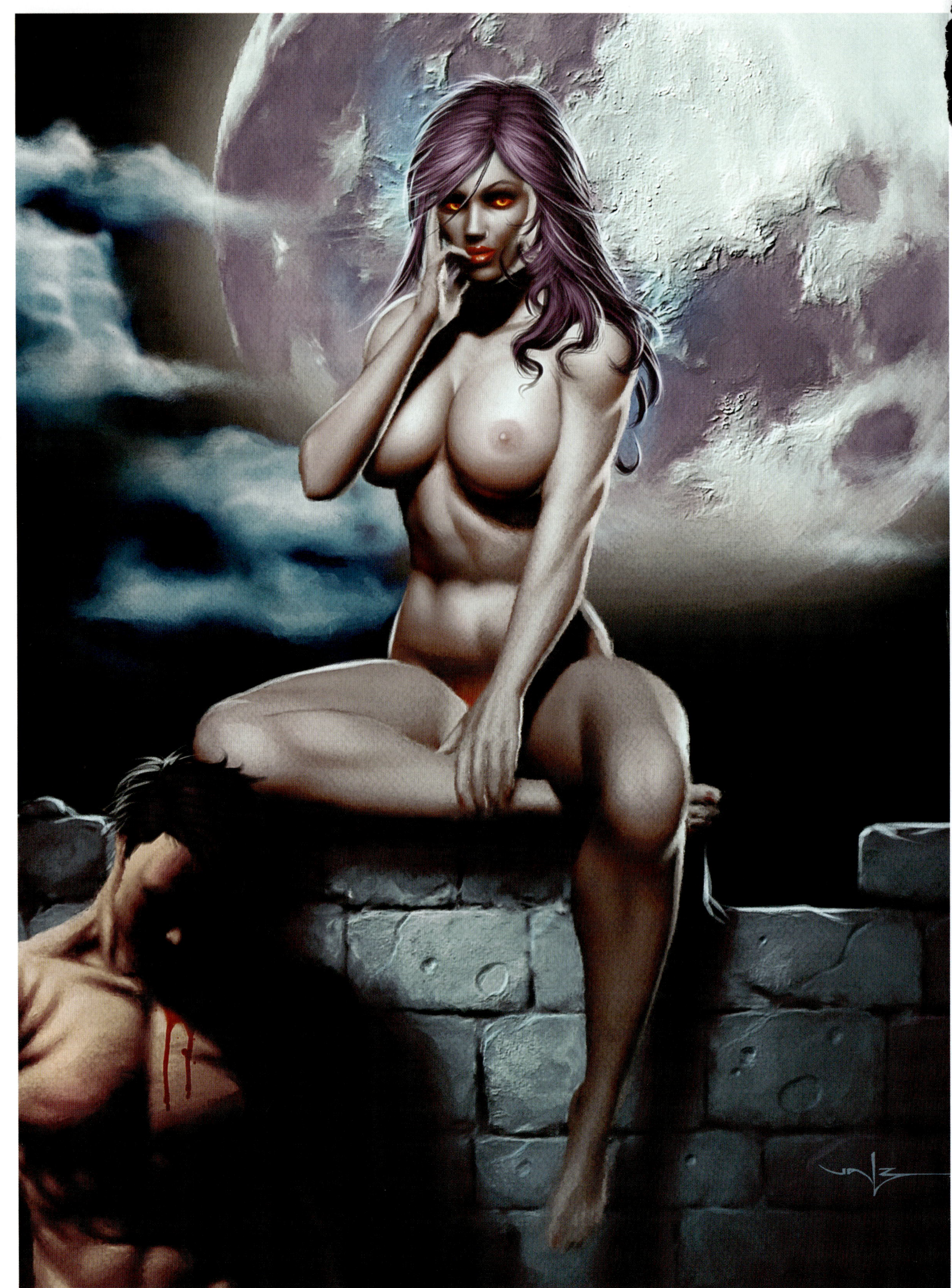

Guilty Pleasure